# YouTube
# WORLD
# RECORDS

# DON'T TRY THIS AT HOME

Some of this book's clips feature stunts performed either by professionals or under the supervision of professionals. Accordingly the publishers must insist that no one attempt to re-create or re-enact any stunt or activity performed on the featured videos.

THIS IS A CARLTON BOOK

Published by Carlton Books Ltd
20 Mortimer Street
London W1T 3JW

Text and design © 2015
Carlton Books Ltd

ISBN 978-1-78097-684-6

Project Editor: Matthew Lowing
Editorial: Caroline Curtis and Chris Parker
Design: James Pople and Darren Jordan
Production: Rachel Burgess
Picture Research: Steve Behan

A CIP catalogue for this book is available from the British Library

Printed in Dubai

10 9 8 7 6 5 4 3 2

# YouTube
# WORLD
# RECORDS

ADRIAN BESLEY

CARLTON
BOOKS

# CONTENTS

# INTRODUCTION

Welcome to the only records book that enables you to see the records being broken for yourself. Enter the short URL or scan the QR code into your tablet, laptop or computer and witness history being made across the world.

The fastest, biggest, highest, thinnest – all over the world people are united by a fascination with human achievements. We all love a record breaker. Whether it is a hundredth of a second being shaved off a famous sporting record or the first recording of a fantastically bizarre new category, we share a fascination with discovering who and what. Till now, the only thing missing has been our chance to actually see the record-breakers in action ...

That's where YouTube comes in. This global resource is open to anyone to upload their videos. It contains literally thousands of record-breaking clips, from the most well-known to the completely obscure. Some have millions of views, while others remain virtually undiscovered.

Among the gems available to view are Usain Bolt's amazing 100-metre sprint; the world's tallest man sharing a coffee with the world's shortest man; Nik Wallenda's nail-biting tightrope (the highest ever while blindfolded); the man who moves bucketfuls of maggots with his mouth; a woman who rubs chilli seeds into her eyes; and the land speed record for a toilet!

This book is your guide to the best of the record-breaking videos on YouTube. It leads you to the most exciting, the most thrilling, the most interesting and the most ridiculous videos on the site. Just read through the brief description and then use the short URL address or the QR code to access the clip – all, of course, completely for free.

# HIGH-FLYING RECORDS

Don't look down! It's time to meet some of the sky-high heroes of the record-breaking world. These are some vertigo-immune daredevils who don't know the meaning of fear.

## Whoops!

http://y2u.be/6PEeKQoN4SI

There aren't many record breakers in this book who set their records unintentionally. Professional skier Fred Syversen is the exception. Syversen is a free skier, skiing off-piste wherever he wants. On this occasion, while being filmed by a helicopter, he chose the wrong line and headed straight over a cliff. He fell a world record 351 feet (107 metres) reaching 100 mph (160 km/h) but landed in snow. He damaged his vital organs but amazingly was fine after a month's recuperation.

RECORD -BREAKING SHALLOW WATER DIVE

## ▶ The Greatest Flop

http://y2u.be/cur0YILfQB8

He's the King of the Belly Flops, the Prince of Paddling Pool Plunges, he's Professor Splash. The Professor (real name: Darren Taylor) claims to be the only diver to have mastered the art of shallow water diving – plunging from great heights into shallow water. Here he is breaking his own world record at the University of Science and Technology in Trondheim, Norway by diving 36 feet (11 metres) into a paddling pool containing just 12 inches (30.5 centimetres) of water.

# On Your Toes

http://y2u.be/cPoZoMZyY2M

Bagjumping is the kind of sport that looks a lot of fun ... until you climb up and realize how far it is to the ground. The sport involves jumping from a platform on a crane onto an inflatable bag on the ground and Daniel Moesl is one of the leading proponents. In Tallinn Estonia in 2013, Moesl performs his "Lucifer double front flip", hanging upside down by his toes, spreading his arms into the death position and falling from a world record 171 feet (52 metres).

# ▶ Wingsuit Wonder

http://y2u.be/N6Zk9GO0ql0

Jhonathan Florez leaped out of a plane above Colombia, in April 2012 and broke four world records in one death-defying jump. Diving from 37,265 feet (11,360 metres), he made the highest ever wingsuit jump and his time of 9 minutes, 6 seconds smashed the record for the longest duration wingsuit jump. He also took the record for greatest horizontal distance flown in a wingsuit – a mammoth 16.315 miles (26.26 kilometres) – and flew the greatest distance ever in a wingsuit of 17.52 miles (28.2 kilometres).

MULTIPLE RECORD BREAKER IN ONE FLIGHT

9

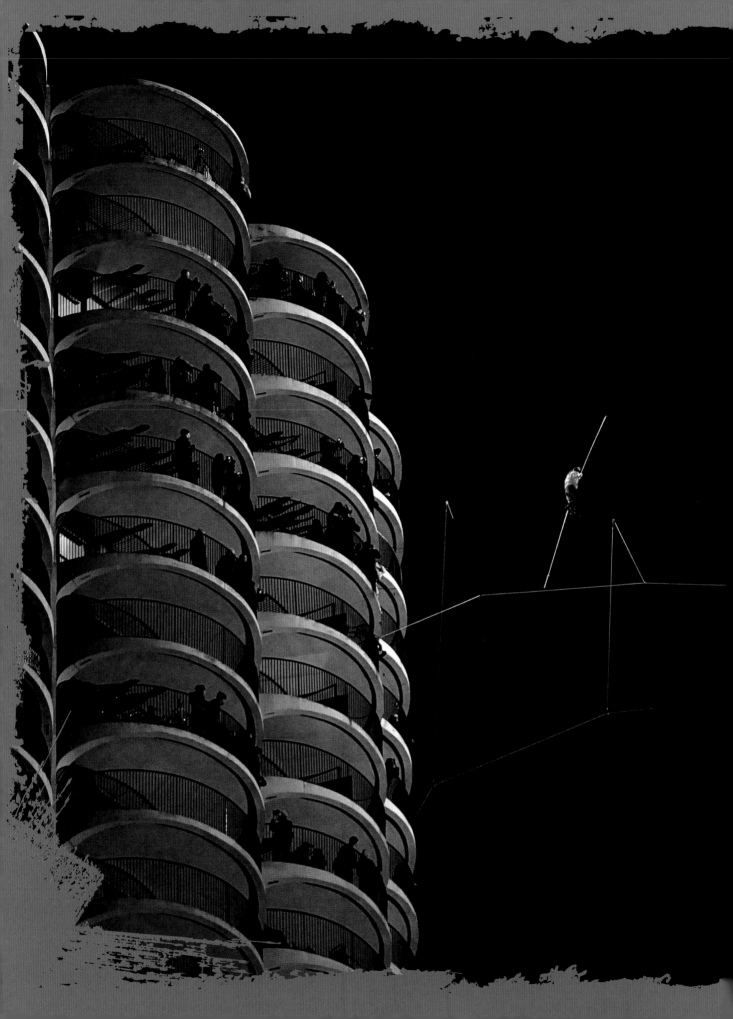

## ▲ Windy City Wire Walk

http://y2u.be/XvzcLs3H5Jk

Despite his great-grandfather Karl falling to his death from a wire in 1978, Nik Wallenda, a seventh-generation tightrope artist, took on the record for the highest blindfolded tightrope walk. Facing winds of 24 mph (39 km/h) and with no safety net or harness, he steps along a wire suspended between Chicago's two Marina City towers. No wonder live TV broadcast the monumental walk with a 10-second delay. Even knowing he makes it, you'll watch it with your heart in your mouth.

**WORLD RECORD FOR BLINDFOLD TIGHTROPE WALK**

# YOUTUBE HITS RECORDS

In 10 years, YouTube has grown to be a part of the daily lives of millions of people. No surprise, then, that it now has its own illustrious record holders.

## ▶ The Song That Broke YouTube

http://youtu.be/9bZkp7q19f0

References to celebrities "breaking the internet" are common these days, but Psy's ubiquitous hit 'Gangnam Style' really did break YouTube. The South Korean singer's catchy ditty continues to break YouTube viewing records (a billion more than the next most watched, Justin Bieber's 'Baby'). In December 2014, Psy's horsey dance hit swept past 2,147,483,647 views, the maximum YouTube could count. Fortunately, the YouTube engineer had seen it coming and updated their counter to a maximum of 9.22 quintillion. How long until 'Gangnam Style' reaches that?

YOUTUBE'S MOST-WATCHED VIDEO

## Soap Opera

http://youtu.be/XpaOjMXyJGk

The most-watched YouTube ad of all time (over 65 million views) is a touching experiment on women's self-image. The film features a screened-off FBI-trained sketch artist drawing a woman's portrait according to her own self-description. He then sketches a portrait of the same woman according to a complete stranger's description of her. The results are then displayed side by side – how they see themselves and how others see them. The results are surprising and reinforce the Real Beauty message of the advertisers, Dove soap.

## Game On

http://y2u.be/X3HON0P6q6c

Ever heard of Felix Kjellberg? He is only the most successful poster and producer on YouTube with around 35 million subscribers. Better known as PewDiePie, he has been uploading videos since 2010 when he was 21 years old. His videos are made up of funny, inane and often expletive-heavy commentaries on video games. Zany, crude and full of energy and shrieks, he comes across as just another player, sharing his experiences in the gaming world. Whatever he has, if you could put it in a bottle, you'd make your fortune.

## Charlie's Finger

http://youtu.be/_OBlgSz8sSM

The Top 20 most-watched videos on YouTube are music videos – with one exception. A clip of two young boys, sitting side by side in an armchair, is right up there with Miley, Justin and Taylor. Dad Howard Davies-Carr uploaded *Charlie Bit My Finger – Again!* to show relatives, but it became a phenomenon. Sweet and cheeky, it's full of infectious laughter, so it's no surprise it has been watched over 700 million times.

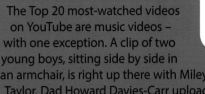

## ▲ 24 Hour People

http://youtu.be/o_v9MY_FMcw

It's called the Best Song Ever, and as far as the records books are concerned it has a claim. The One Direction video for the song was watched 10.9 million times in its first day online, beating Miley Cyrus's record for Most Views in 24 Hours. The video finds Harry, Liam, Zayn, Niall and Louis in a playful sketch as executives discussing the band's new image before breaking out to perform their hit track. That was enough to send the Directioneers around the world clicking Repeat Play again and again.

**HIGHEST ONE-DAY VIEWING FIGURES**

# SPEED AND ACCURACY

Another selection of quick on the draw records. Here accuracy is just as important as speed; one false move could mean death, a dodgy haircut or a customer questioning their receipt.

## ▶ A Throwaway Record

http://y2u.be/JriUEsRk8Ns

The Great Throwdini is undoubtedly the world's greatest knife thrower. Despite only taking up knife throwing at the age of 50, the Reverend Doctor David R. Adamovich (his real name) has set or broken 40 world records in throwing and catching knives and bullets. He has thrown ten 14-inch (36-centimetre) knives around a human target in just 4.29 seconds and 102 knives in one minute, and he even flings the blades while wearing a blindfold!

## ▼ Around the World in 60 Seconds

http://y2u.be/6o9GVDIlZLE

**THE ONE-MINUTE GLOBE TROTTER**

The Indian subcontinent is a hotbed of record breaking. We travel to Hyderabad, India for this impressive feat of both memory and delivery as Rahamath Ali names all 199 countries in exactly one minute. You may be pedantic about the number of countries there are in the world (some say 193, others take the total over 200) and about how clearly Rahamath pronounces each country (you can definitely hear "Mongolia!"), but he reels them off in a mesmeric performance.

# Supermarket Sweep

http://y2u.be/NeVrYrTbnm4

It might be best not to watch this if you are one of those shoppers who gets frustrated at a super slow supermarket checkout. This shows just how fast it can be done if your shop assistant at the till isn't chatting, searching for the barcode or entering the number by hand. Ben Clarke and Samantha Wroe scanned and neatly bagged 50 items – varying from crisps to cordials to a bag of sugar – in 1 minute, 19 seconds.

## THE WORLD'S FASTEST HAIRCUT

## A Quick Trim

http://y2u.be/InWd1aasLps

I bet the next time you pop to the barbers for a quick trim it won't be anything like this one. Roberto Gangale of Carlo's Barbershop in Cleveland, Ohio failed with his first attempt to beat 55 seconds, but luckily his local mayor took the chair and was finished in just 49.76 seconds. And this wasn't just a buzz cut: to break the record it had to be an accurate, "businessman haircut", which includes trimming at least a half-inch (1.25 centimetres) around the head.

# ▼ Shear Brilliance

http://y2u.be/TbUDbH6tjGs

Spare a thought for the poor sheep in this clip. One moment she's nice and warm in a big woolly coat ... then wham! Less than 15 seconds later, she's stripped down to the skin. She had no chance against New Zealand's living legend, David Fagan – who has been called "the Pelé of sheep shearing". Eleven times a world record holder, he can shear a sheep faster than most men can shave .

## THE FASTEST SHEEP SHEARER IN THE WORLD

# THE NEED FOR SPEED!

Whoosh! There's no substitute for pure lightning strike speed and these guys have all taken the needle into the red with power, guts and a little madness ...

## ▶ Lightning Bolt

http://y2u.be/3nbjhpcZ9_g

It was a the year after the Beijing Olympics. Gold medallist Usain Bolt had lost weeks of training after a car accident. He claimed to be just 85 per cent fit weeks before the race and talk was of a slow track in Berlin. And yet, the Jamaican almost effortlessly broke his own 100 metres record by an amazing eleven hundreths of a second. Even his competitors could not quite believe it. Asafa Powell, who finished in third place, said that "even after the finish I couldn't catch him".

THE FASTEST 100M SPRINT ON RECORD

## ▶ Smash!

http://y2u.be/7HTeG0CmKbU

For all the power of the tennis serve and the intensity of the squash shot, badminton is the real seat of power among racket sports. Tennis serves reach 160 mph (258 km/h), squash pushes the limit to 170 mph (274 km/h), but badminton smashes regularly break the 200 mph (322 km/h) barrier. Chinese player Fu Hai Feng (with his partner Cai Yun) is the world men's badminton doubles champion and king of the smash. His 2005 record of 206 mph (332 km/h) has been beaten in racket promotional videos but never in real competition.

16

## ▼ Two-Wheeled Triumph

http://y2u.be/PP-7WX12H2I

They call him the Red Baron, but the only things Éric shoots down are world records. Daredevil Éric possesses the land speed cycling record on both snow and gravel. He hit a speed of 107 mph (172 km/h) on the gravel slopes of the Cerro Negro volcano in Nicaragua moments before crashing and breaking several ribs. He then opted for the softer landing of snow and recorded a speed of 138 mph (222 km/h) in Les Arcs ski resort in the French Alps.

THE FASTEST
BIKE ON SNOW
AND GRAVEL

## ▼ Olympic Hero

http://y2u.be/2f7HFT2tvcQ

"We knew what we were witnessing ... To see the record broken was special enough. But that race was the best I have ever seen." So commented Olympic champion, Steve Cram. David Rudisha's 800 metres was the standout athletic performance of the London Olympics. Considered to be one of the prize records in athletics, the record for 800 metres has been held by only four men since 1976. At the age of just 23, Kenya's David Rudisha had broken it for an astonishing third time.

## In a Spin

http://y2u.be/_YBCOv43h98

It would be reasonable to assume that the holder of a basketball spinning record would be a Harlem Globetrotter, but the Blindfolded Simultaneous Basketball Spinning record is held by a cop! When Michael Kettman isn't patrolling the downtown area of St Augustine, Florida, he's busy practising spinning his balls. Michael was inspired by the Globetrotters legend Curly Neal to try spinning and discovered he was a natural. He also holds the record for the non-blindfold simultaneous basketball spinning – an amazing 28 balls!

# EXTREME WEATHER

Witness the shock and devastation brought by these record-breaking natural disasters – hurricanes, tsunamis and other calamitous events – in tense and dramatic footage uploaded to YouTube.

## ▶ Weather Report

http://y2u.be/unV5KcSrY-I

This clip went viral and became known as the *Hurricane Charley Gas Station* video. It shows a petrol station in Charlotte Harbor, Florida being torn apart by winds of over 155 mph (249 km/h). Hurricane Charley, classed as Category 4 (the second strongest band), was the strongest hurricane to hit southwest Florida for 50 years. These winds were the strongest ever caught on video and were captured by Mike Theiss, whose brilliant weather films appear on the Ultimate Chase channel.

## The Super Tsunami

http://y2u.be/yN6EgMMrhdI

On 9 July 1958, an earthquake caused a landslide at the head of Lituya Bay in Alaska. It generated a mega-tsunami measuring between 100 feet (30 metres) and 300 feet (91 metres), the highest tsunami wave in recorded history. This fascinating four-minute BBC clip tells the story of the tsunami, illuminated by the incredible tale of two witnesses, the only survivors from the boats out that day. It has been viewed over 5 million times.

# ▶ Hailstone from Hell

http://y2u.be/w47HxYgG7bg

The hailstones that fell in Vivian, South Dakota in 2010 weren't unpleasant, they were downright dangerous. As massive ice balls pummelled the ground and houses, locals described it as like having someone throw bricks from an airplane. After the storm, Les Scott picked the largest hailstone to put in his daquiri, then thought better of it. He contacted the National Weather Service who revealed that both the weight – 1.9375 pounds (31 ounces, 880 grams) and the circumference – 18.5 inches (44.5 centimetres) made it a record breaker.

THE LARGEST LANDSLIDE IN HISTORY

# ▲ Mount Devastation

http://y2u.be/IhU6jml6NY4

Mount St Helens is a volcano in the US state of Washington. In 1980 an earthquake caused the north face to slide away, creating the largest landslide ever recorded. The landslide triggered explosions that sent rocks, ash, volcanic gas and steam into the air at over 300 mph (483 km/h) and created a column of ash that reached more than 15 miles (24 kilometres) into the atmosphere in only 15 minutes. This video, created from a series of photographs, reveals the enormity of this colossal act of nature.

# AMAZING ANIMAL RECORDS

The animal kingdom has its champions too. A safari through YouTube's wildlife clips reveals some fascinating and surprising records and some incredible footage from the wild world.

## ▶ Monkey Business

http://y2u.be/zsXP8qeFF6A

About 98 per cent of their genome is identical to humans, so it is not surprising that chimpanzees are regarded as the cleverest of animal species. They can make and use tools, hunt in organized groups and have shown they are capable of empathy, altruism and self-awareness. Over and above all this, they are adept at computer skills – and in the case of Ayumu, featured in this video, can beat a human at memory games.

CHIMP WITH A MEMORY SUPERIOR TO HUMANS

## ◀ Here Be Dragons

http://y2u.be/q7CQInAXoqY

The Komodo dragon, a type of monitor lizard found on only five islands in southeastern Indonesia, wins the prize for being the largest living lizard in the world. The male Komodos grow to an amazing 10 feet (3 metres) long and weigh up to 176 pounds (80 kilograms). They are powerful creatures and it's no surprise to discover they are fearsome hunters executing lightning attacks, with shark-like sharp teeth and saliva full of deadly bacteria. And yes, they have been known to attack humans!

# ▼ Who Are You Calling Dumbo?

http://y2u.be/iPdGYVNd2qQ

As the largest of the elephant species, the African elephant takes the honour of the planet's biggest land animal. It measures up to 24 feet (7.3 metres) in length , 13 feet (3.96 metres) in height and can weigh up to 11 tons. Despite this they can get around at a fair speed and can outpace an average human over a short distance. This entertaining clip illustrates that as one of these creatures decides to give chase to a reporter who comes too close.

**THE LARGEST ANIMAL ON DRY LAND**

# ▲ Dive Bomb

http://y2u.be/rz0_Q8Tsxuk

Most people would quickly name the cheetah as the fastest creature on earth, but the fastest creature on the planet? The answer is the Peregrine Falcon. Its horizontal cruising speeds reach to just 50–65 mph (80–100 km/h), but when it is in a hunting dive, known as a stoop, this bird of prey regularly flies over 150 mph (240 km/h), more than twice the speed of the cheetah, and has been recorded at 242 mph (389 km/h). They plunge at such a rate that they usually kill their prey with a single blow.

# Big Fish

http://y2u.be/dUMUSFLyZpU

The Whale Shark is the largest fish in the sea. It lives in the warm waters of the planet's tropical seas. They grow to around the size of a school bus – the largest ever caught was 41 feet (12 metres) long although they are thought to grow even bigger than that. Fortunately they are not predators; they are docile animals, often letting swimmers hitch a lift, but they are an endangered species, hunted in parts of Asia.

# FREAKY FOOD RECORDS

The world of food and drink showcases some marvellous records, including enormous vegetables, oversized fast food and a time-honoured crazy method of cracking open champagne bottles.

## ▶ How's That for a Hot Dog?

http://y2u.be/SfA_L_zfqiU

For those with a bigger than normal appetite, the Big Hot Dog might be the answer. The Chicago-based company make the biggest commercially available hot dog in the world – a massive 40 times bigger than usual hot dog sausages. It is 16 inches (41 centimetres) long and 4 inches (10 centimetres) in diameter. It weighs 7 pounds (3.1 kilograms) and costs just $169.99 – with a giant bun and relish included. What's more, the company has a very entertaining infomercial ...

## Rolling in Dough

http://y2u.be/xNkdDGdrSFE

South Korea is not a country renowned for its pizza, but it is home to Lee Moon Ky, the World Champion Pizza Freestyler. Lee is as much an entertainer as a pizza chef. His world record saw him rolling a pizza 38 times along the back of his shoulders in 30 seconds – a unique throwing trick. This stunning video shows him performing this and various other pizza spinning tricks at the 2014 World Pizza Games.

## Super Sabre

http://y2u.be/k_vfg1dJito

Napoleon is reputed to have declared: "Champagne! In victory one deserves it; in defeat one needs it." It was his troops who first popularized "sabring" champagne bottles – severing the neck from the bottle with the flat edge of a sabre. It is a precise skill – cutting through the glass at an exact stress point – and is one perfected by Mitch Ancoana as he opens a world record 34 bottles in a minute. An achievement worth celebrating.

## ▼ Onion King

http://y2u.be/ZCIfa3L0dtY

Tony Glover was named King of the Onions when he managed to produce a mighty onion weighing 18 pounds 11 ounces (8.5 kilograms). Using seeds bought from the previous record holder, Peter Glazebrook, Tony says it took nearly a year to grow his mighty specimen. He gives them nitrogen-rich food and ensures the humidity is just right. Giant onions have trebled in size since 1985 and word has it that the holy grail of onions – the 20-pounder (9 kilograms) – is just around the corner.

THE WORLD'S LARGEST ONION

## ◄ Pizza the Action

http://y2u.be/IT09m7mOItM

In front of 6,000 cheering spectators, Pali Grewal, a pizza chef in south London, made three large pizzas in 39.1 seconds – a pizza every 13 seconds. The contestants at the competition had to hand stretch fresh dough, spread the tomato sauce and top three large pizzas – one pepperoni, one mushroom and one cheese. Quality was scrutinized as two judges inspected each aspect of the process. If the pizza was not perfect, it was returned to the competitor to be remade.

THE FASTEST PIZZA MAKER IN THE WORLD

# RECORD-BREAKING PEOPLE

Those born at the extremes of the physical spectrum – the tallest, the smallest, etc. – have always held a special fascination. These clips reveal the human beings behind some of the statistics.

## ▶ A Tall Story

http://y2u.be/RwzMWuAxANw

Robert Pershing Wadlow from Alton, Illinois, USA is the tallest recorded person ever to have lived. He was born in 1918 and by the time he was eight years old he was 6 feet 2 inches (1.88 metres) tall. By the time he was 19 he had reached a height of 8 feet 11.1 inches (2.72 metres) – the tallest living man is a mere 8 feet 4 inches (2.54 metres). Unfortunately, Robert would only live a few years more after an infection in his foot spread to his body. He was known as the Gentle Giant and over 27,000 people attended his funeral.

## Tallest / Smallest

http://y2u.be/bKnk1OlzqvY

13 November 2014 saw a unique occasion in record history. In the shadow of London's Tower Bridge, the world's tallest man met the world's smallest man – for the first time ever! To celebrate the 60th anniversary of the Guinness World Records, Sultan Kösen from Turkey, who stands at 8 feet 9 inches (2.51 metres), was introduced to Chandra Bahadur Dangi from Nepal, who measures 21.5 inches (55 centimetres). And, that's about the long and the short of it!

THE TALLEST MAN WHO EVER LIVED

## ◀ Animal Magnetism

http://y2u.be/rbUuzCRa3Ug

Former kick-boxing coach Etibar Elchyev from Georgia is known as "Magnetic Man". Ever since he discovered his ability to attract metal objects to his body, Etibar has been setting new records. Here, in December 2013, we find him putting spoons on his chest and back – 53 in total, a new world record. An excellent talent, but he must dread visiting the cafeteria. Scientists claim his skin is not magnetic but merely "sticky". Whatever ... he's still in a magnetic field of his own!

## ▶ Inseparable Brothers

http://y2u.be/gPcijt2WaIs

Twin brothers Ronnie and Donnie Galyon were born healthy in Dayton, Ohio, in October 1951. Joined at the waist, they each had arms, legs and separate hearts but shared a stomach and some organs. Sixty-three years later they were still joined and could celebrate being the eldest-ever conjoined twins, beating Italian brothers Giacomo and Giovanni Battista Tocci, who were born in Italy in 1877. The twins spent their lives from the age of four in circus sideshows but have now retired to live with their younger brother.

# WILD AND WACKY

Hidden away in the nooks and corners of YouTube are some odd and eccentric records. Here are just a few ...

## ◢ Sealed with a Kiss

https://www.youtube.com/watch?v=WJWbg2X5I14

THE LONGEST KISS IN HISTORY

A married couple, Ekkachai and Laksana Tiranarat, locked lips for 46 hours, 24 minutes in a kissathon contest in Pattaya, Thailand. They were the winners from 14 competing couples, who were all required to have a marriage certificate or a letter from both parents. It wasn't all for love, though: they were competing for a diamond ring and a cash prize! And to really ruin the romance ... they were allowed to eat, drink and use the lavatory, provided they did not break their embrace.

## Cup Winner

http://y2u.be/RsBdA2S2E-8

Sport stacking is a game in which competitors stack plastic cups in specific sequences as quickly as possible. The toughest of the disciplines is the "cycle" in which 12 cups are stacked in three different ways, including pyramid formations. Fifteen-year-old William Orrell is the indisputable king of stacking – holding the record for all three individual disciplines. This clip shows his incredible record-breaking cycle stack at the first-ever Nation's Capital Open Sport Stacking Tournament where he takes just 5.100 seconds to finish.

# ◄ Up the Wall

http://y2u.be/OxL-RHi42gU

Speed wall climbing is a growing sport around the world and could soon receive Olympic status. It is explosive and exciting and has its own star in Ukrainian Danylo Boldyrev. He is the Usain Bolt of the speed climbing wall, an unstoppable force. At the men's speed event of Climbing World Championship 2014, he smashed 13 hundredths of a second off the world record. That is a pretty huge margin when you consider it took him only 5.6 seconds to scale the 49-foot (15-metre) wall.

**RECORD-BREAKING WALL CLIMBER**

# ► Dead Cool

http://y2u.be/xtHzRjnoXKw

In November 2014 in Mexico City, 509 slightly scary-looking skeletons in ball gowns and brimmed hats gathered in the city centre to set the world record for the largest gathering of Catrinas. The figure of Catrina, known as the Elegant Death, was created and immortalized in works by artists Guadalupe Posada and Diego Rivera and is now a traditional part of Mexico's Day of the Dead celebrations. People dress as the skeletal character to visit cemeteries and share offerings and food with the dead and their families.

**A RECORD GATHERING OF CATRINAS**

# SPORTS RECORD BREAKERS

There's more to sport than winning. There are records to be broken. These guys have etched their names in the history of their sports – however strange!

## ▶ It's a Long Shot

http://y2u.be/7kV4-ziw4pU

Harlem Globetrotter Corey "Thunder" Law scored the longest basketball shot of all time in 2014. The 23-year-old hurled the amazing basket from deep in the seats at the far end of the Phoenix Suns' US Airways Arena. Battling it out with two of his teammates, Corey was the only one to succeed as he added over 5 feet (1.52 metres) to the existing record in a throw of 109 feet 9 inches (33.45 metres) from the hoop. Incredibly, Corey holds the backward throwing record too (see page 54).

WORLD RECORD-BREAKING BASKET

## Xtreme 19th

http://y2u.be/iOWR7O1oSgU

The Legend Golf 18-hole course in South Africa has a bonus hole – the "Xtreme 19th" – the highest and longest par three golf hole in the world. The tee sits on top of a cliff on Hanglip Mountain, more than 1,400 feet (427 metres) above a green carved in the shape of the continent of Africa – it takes nearly 30 seconds for the ball to hit the ground. Drill a hole-in-one and you win $1 million, but no one has yet bettered a two-shot birdie.

http://y2u.be/1wVho3I0NtU

## ◀ Maradona Miracle

The best football goal ever is, of course, a matter of opinion. Few, however, could disagree that Maradona's thrilling second goal against England in the 1986 World Cup quarter final deserves its place in history. Four minutes earlier the mercurial Argentinian had already scored his notorious "Hand of God" goal, but this one relied on nothing but his magical feet. The legendary live commentary by Uruguayan Victor Hugo Morales only adds to the wonder as Maradona pirouettes, slaloms and dummies his way to goal.

**THE WORLD'S GREATEST GOAL**

## High Heel Hotfoot

http://y2u.be/WJ2DC2X1e5k

Running in high heels can be a risky operation. You can end up with a broken heel or a sprained ankle. Not Julia Plecher, though. In a 100-metre sprint, all the stiletto-clad teenager from Germany broke was a world record. She really does cut a dash, running the distance in under 15 seconds despite wearing a figure-hugging outfit that matches her gold high heels. Keep watching and you'll see Julia triumph in a stiletto race in Berlin – wearing an 8.5-centimetre (3.3-inch) heel!

## ▶ Throwing Her Weight Around

http://y2u.be/TojYpZhQyxQ

Officially awarded the title of the World's Heaviest Sportswoman, Sharran Alexander is Britain's most successful international Sumo Wrestler. Sharran took up Sumo in 2006 only after her children put her name down for a TV challenge show, but she has already won four gold medals in international tournaments. A 2nd Kyu grade wrestler, she weighed in at 32 stone (203.2 kilograms), twice the weight of a male heavyweight boxer, but admitted she had "let herself go a bit".

**THE WORLD'S HEAVIEST SPORTSWOMAN**

# THEME PARK RECORDS

Scream if you want to go faster! Actually it isn't possible to go any faster than on some of these record-breaking rides – but you may find yourself screaming anyway.

**TALLEST ROLLER-COASTER – FOR NOW**

## ▼ Viennese Whirl

http://y2u.be/UATJDA35wXk

All this speed and spinning getting too much for you? Come with us to Vienna, the capital of Austria, famous for Mozart, cake ... and a chairoplane 384 feet (117 metres) high! The Prater Turm (tower) is as high as a 33-storey building from which fun-seekers "fly" at a speed of 37 mph (60 km/h). The world's highest-flying swing ride floats its guests on a seat that would easily clear the Statue of Liberty's torch and Big Ben's clock tower spire and gives them a spinning vista of the city.

**THE WORLD'S TALLEST SWING RIDE**

## Big Daddy

http://y2u.be/xTNcnJS-a2M

The Kingda Ka ride in the Six Flags Great Adventure park in New Jersey is the daddy of rollercoaster rides. It just lost its fastest coaster status to the Formula Rossa ride and is set to lose its tallest status to the Skyscraper "Polecaster" in Florida in 2017, but it is still a thrilling ride. It races from zero to 128 mph (206 km/h) in 3.5 seconds, plummets 418 feet (127 metres) and enters into a 270-degree vertical spiral, inducing weightlessness and a few queasy stomachs.

## ▼ Vomit Comet

http://y2u.be/qqN9PDS3hOc

People have been known to queue for over four hours to ride for just 2 minutes, 45 seconds on The Smiler at Alton Towers, a theme park in the UK. It is the rollercoaster with the most inversions (turning riders upside down and back again) in the world. There are 14 different inversions of seven different kinds from the common corkscrew, cobra and dive-loops to the rarer double batwing and sea-serpent twists. Confused? Never mind, climb aboard and hold tight!

## Fast Formula

http://y2u.be/ijuQwnfBBZw

The Formula Rossa rollercoaster in Abu Dhabi's Ferrari World boasts acceleration from 0 to 60 mph (96 km/h) in just two seconds and reaches a world record 149 mph (240 km/h). In 2010, Felipe Massa and Fernando Alonso, Formula One motor racing drivers, took their seats in the fastest rollercoaster on the planet. Now, while their bodies are used to being flung around at ridiculously high speeds, their faces are usually encased in helmets. Just watch as the g-force hits these seasoned speed merchants.

RECORD-BREAKING TWISTS ON A ROLLER-COASTER

# SCARY AND SHOCKING!

Delve into the lucky dip of the world of records and who knows what'll emerge. You could find some hair-raising danger, interesting collections and sometimes, something truly, truly bizarre.

## ▼ Rocky Road

http://y2u.be/zGA3qXQs1wE

The North Yungas Road in Bolivia is 43 miles (69 kilometres) long and 2,000 feet (610 metres) high, and claims around 300 lives a year. No wonder it is called the Death Road. Perils along the Most Dangerous Road in the World include rock avalanches, fog and trucks squeezing by each other on its loose stone surface. Often a single track 10 feet (3 metres) wide, it has no guard rails, just sheer drops down the cliff edges. The route does, however, offer some stunning scenery.

DEATH ROAD –
WORLD'S MOST
DANGEROUS

## Beat the Record

http://y2u.be/Q9FrW-Wr-ds

It was one of those records they thought might never be beaten. The mighty feat of drumming 1,203 beats in a minute had stood for eight years and despite many attempts by the world's best it had not been surpassed. Tom "Tommy Gun" Grosset had himself failed with previous attempts, but this time he was in the zone and added another five beats to the record. If you like Tom's style, check out his other YouTube videos – he does some mean drum covers of well-known film soundtracks.

## Say Aaaaah!

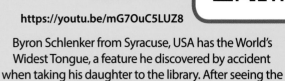

https://youtu.be/mG7OuC5LUZ8

Byron Schlenker from Syracuse, USA has the World's Widest Tongue, a feature he discovered by accident when taking his daughter to the library. After seeing the widest tongue in a book, Schlenker wondered how his licker measured up. After official measuring, it transpired that his tongue was indeed a record breaker at 3.27 inches (8.3 centimetres) wide. Although Byron seems to be enjoying the celebrity, his family are less impressed: "I honestly think it's weird. I mean, who wouldn't think that?" said his daughter.

## Big Deal

http://y2u.be/jZnekqb0qQU

Try this one at home with a pack of cards. You need to deal 52 cards into four separate piles. All the cards in each pile need to touch another card in the pile and there has to be clear space between each of the piles. World record holder Paul Brooks dealt out a whole deck of cards in just 14.7 seconds. And don't forget that if you accidentally flip Mr Bun the Baker over, you have to start again.

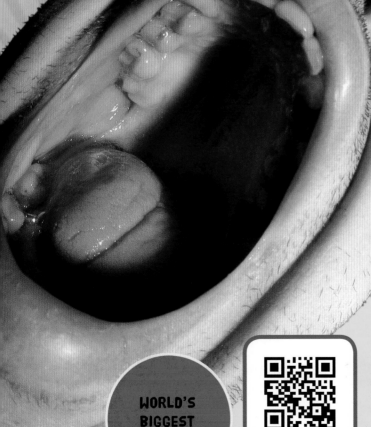

WORLD'S BIGGEST MOUTH

## ◀ Mighty Mouth

https://youtu.be/CimpFIxLhfw

"Big Mouth" is usually a term of abuse, but for Francisco Domingo Joaquim aka Chiquinho from Angola it is the greatest accolade. For the man nicknamed The Angolan Jaw of Awe really does have the biggest mouth in the world. His elastic lips and mouth have been measured at 6.69 inches (17 centimetres) at full gape. That's room for Chiquinho to fit in a can of drink sideways, spin it around inside his mouth and gulp it out again!

# DON'T TRY THIS AT HOME!

How desperate can you be to get your name in the record books? These record breakers seem to feel no pain as they take one or more of their senses to the limit.

## Spice of Life

http://y2u.be/MhfobnpvhnA

Since childhood Anandita Dutta Tamuly has had a passion for the hot pepper. She has set a record by eating 20 ghost peppers in a minute and another for eight jalapenos in the same time. Filming for his show, top chef Gordon Ramsay found that one bite into a red-hot Naga jolokia was enough, but Anandita ate 51 of them (nine short of her record) and then, incredibly, broke a record by rubbing the seeds of 24 of them into her eyes!

**MOST NUMBER OF PEGS ON FACE**

## ▶ Peg Face

http://y2u.be/pS2AszO0z44

We've all got a skill lurking somewhere, it's just a matter of finding it. Kelvin "The Peg Man" Mercado, 36 years old, discovered he had a unique talent for clipping clothes pegs on his face. Now he's a world record holder. Pegs are attached in neat formation to every loose, and not so loose, piece of skin as well as to his lips and nose. Altogether he managed to clip on 163 pegs – and it makes for quite a sight.

## ▼ Saucy Drinker

http://y2u.be/xNH75yom-fM

"Well done, Dad!" says a voice off camera as Charles Rawles polishes off the last of three bottles of the red-hot Tabasco sauce in just 30 seconds. This is no polished TV show performance but a home video to prove Charles is the record breaker when it comes to drinking the incredibly spicy sauce. Now, Charles doesn't look in a great way after drinking his way through three bottles, but his son's well impressed – and surely that's worth something?

## Tastes a Little Sharp?

http://y2u.be/zUeUpAhq4Gw

This is complete madness. Consuming even the smallest piece of glass can kill a person. It can wound the mouth, throat, stomach, intestines and bowels as it passes through the digestive system. And yet 22-year-old Potesh Talukdar from Assam, India seems to have no problem seeing off a whole cocktail glass full of glass accompanied only by some lemon juice. Amazingly, he does it all in just 1 minute, 27 seconds. If you want to skip to the action it starts around 6.00 minutes into the clip.

## ▶ A Burning Ambition

http://y2u.be/vZjMC6LBt_k

Colin Decker, a Canadian stuntman based in Vancouver, British Columbia, Canada, is the burning man. He holds the world record for having his body on fire for the longest time. Decker uses a special fire-barrier gel that acts like an asbestos suit, preventing even the hairs on the body from being singed. He claims to experience an increasing warmth, but no actual burns. Only when his clothes begin to disintegrate and fall off does he call it a day and collapse into a pool of water.

LONGEST TIME IN FLAMES

# THIRST-QUENCHING RECORDS

It's not just drinking the liquid stuff quickly (although, boy can they guzzle!), but shaking it, sucking it, carrying it and even performing mass scientific experiments with it!

## Lager Top

http://y2u.be/1_e9oTrrf6E

It can be difficult enough getting through the bar with three pints in your hands, so a round of applause is surely due for Oliver Struempfel. He works at the traditional Gillemoos beer festival in the Bavarian town of Abensberg and managed to carry a record 27 one-litre steins of lager. The effort won Oliver the competition to carry as many full mugs as possible over a distance of 40 metres (130 feet). No mean feat considering the total weight exceeds 60 kilograms (132 pounds, about the same as a small adult).

## Longest Straw

http://y2u.be/0deCUB3eYko

Mel Sampson, Afternoon Drive Host on 89.3 K-Rock in New Minas, NS, Canada has a tradition of breaking world records every year. The "Longest Straw" record is one of her favourites. This is the third time she has broken this world record, having taken it from an initial 14.3 feet (4.36 metres) to this incredible 248.8 feet (75.82 metres). After joining 300 straws together, Mel put one end in a can and sucked for over an hour until the cola reached her mouth.

## ▶ Who Flairs Wins

http://y2u.be/JzpHoNBeN9w

Bartending is a real skill. No, not noticing who was at the bar first or pouring a decent pint of Guinness, but in entertaining and thrilling an audience. Flair bartending is the craft of manipulating cocktail shakers and bottles – a highly skilled and entertaining combination of juggling and drink mixing. Tom Dyer is the go-to guy for cocktail flairing. He is a world champion and holds the records for most hand stalls and consecutive bumps on the elbow.

**CHAMPION FLAIR BARTENDER**

## ▲ A Splash of Cola

http://y2u.be/uQ05eALMBEo

As every schoolchild knows mentos and cola make for the best science lesson ever. No one remembers the point, but if all goes well they create a terrific fountain. Over 500 Cincinnatians gathered in the city's Fountain Square in 2007 to launch the largest number of Mentos Geysers to be set off at once in one location. The splash-off was synchronized, leading to an fabulous spray of cola – and a sticky mess in the middle of town.

## ▼ Milking It

http://y2u.be/kBFugzV1KxI

Kobayashi again (see page 107) showing his awesome power of consumption. Here he is at Uncle Bob's Self Storage in Upper Saddle River, New Jersey tipping a gallon – that's eight pints! – of milk down his gullet in just 20 seconds. According to the clip's description, Kobayashi had set a record of eating 13 cupcakes in a minute, "so he needed to wash it down". Considering human stomachs are said to be able to contain around six pints, it's difficult to imagine where it is all going.

## Champion Guzzler

http://y2u.be/EmZGzoRXPP0

Over a million people have watched this amazing display on YouTube. The short clip features a Japanese TV show where Ken Domon from Hokkaido chugs down a 1.5-litre (50 fluid ounce) bottle of water in less than five seconds. It takes a lot of skill just to get the water out of the bottle in that time. Watch for the briefest pause as he lets the bottle expand before crushing it again, and forcing the last few gulps out.

# THE BIGGEST!

When it comes to record breaking, size is definitely important. The Biggest ... is always one of the most popular of the records categories. Here are a few colossal contributors ...

## Bookmark

http://y2u.be/j4NACDLRqml

*Bhutan: A Visual Odyssey Across the Last Himalayan Kingdom* is a book 7 feet (2.13 metres) by 5 feet (1.52 metres). This, the World's Biggest Book, is a result of Michael Hawley's research at the Massachusetts Institute of Technology, where he led expeditions capturing a photographic record of Bhutan. It took 24 hours to print each copy and in total used a gallon of ink on a roll of paper longer than a football field. Only 500 copies were published.

## ▶ Egg-straordinary!

http://y2u.be/aNUW6DL7LXw

The largest bird egg ever seen was put up for sale at Christie's auction house in 2013 and fetched £66,675 pounds ($101,813) at auction. The elephant bird egg is 1 foot (30.5 centimetres) long and nearly 9 inches (22.9 centimetres) in diameter – around 100 times larger than the average chicken's egg. Extinct since the seventeenth century, elephant birds were found only on the island of Madagascar. Flightless, ostrich-like birds, they grew up to 11 feet (3.35 metres) tall.

**THE WORLD'S BIGGEST EGG**

## ▶ Ball Breaker

http://y2u.be/dHNvScJ5bzl

It's a rubber band ball that needs a crane to lift it! Back in 2004, Joel Waul of Florida, USA had a small golf ball-sized sphere of rubber bands. He added to them, and then added more until he had built this 4.5 ton (10,000 pound), multi-coloured, world-record-beating, ball in his driveway five years later. Waul's ball is 6 feet 3 inches (1.9 metres) high, has a circumference of 23 feet 9 inches (7.24 metres) and is made up of more than 300,000 bands.

THE WORLD'S BIGGEST RUBBER-BAND BALL

THE WORLD'S BIGGEST SWIMMING POOL

## ▲ Fancy a Dip?

http://y2u.be/p4tLAgYUpZk

It would probably take a good swimmer 40 minutes or so to swim a length of the swimming pool at San Alfonso del Mar resort at Algarrobo, on Chile's southern coast. This man-made saltwater pool is more than 1,000 yards (1 kilometre) long, covers 20 acres (8 hectares) and holds 66 million gallons of water – that's about 40 times as big as your local pool. It is even heated by the sun to around 80°F (26.5°C) – a good deal warmer than the surrounding ocean.

# THE MORE, THE MERRIER!

Ah mass participation! A chance to meet other bizarrely dressed folk, to stretch your legs in unison at a stadium or to dance slightly out of step alongside hundreds of others ...

## The Tennessee Wave

http://y2u.be/H0K2dvB-7WY

The Mexican Wave – a progression of seated audience members rising to their feet with their hands in the air – is a stadium phenomenon usually perpetrated by bored spectators deciding to make their own entertainment. Just occasionally it can be stunning in its own right. In 2008 the NASCAR short track stadium in Bristol, Tennessee hosted "the Sharpie 500" Sprint Cup. Before the action even got started they were attempting the human wave.
All 160,000 of them!

## ▼ Zombie Apocalypse (almost)

http://y2u.be/QkqC6Fni2KE

They bill the Zombie Pub Crawl as the World's Greatest Undead Party with brain-eating competitions, live pop acts, a "Trapped in the Closet Sing-Along" and a zombie fun run! Minneapolis have been hosting the living dead (or people dressed up as them) annually since 2005. The original 500 zombies have multiplied until, in 2014, over 15,000 grown adults were officially counted stumbling around in a stupefied manner. It was the official record for a zombie gathering.

RECORD-BREAKING NUMBER OF ZOMBIES

## ▶ Crowd Thriller

http://y2u.be/FgYbyV15yzU

On what would have been Michael Jackson's fifty-first birthday, his Mexican fans performed the greatest mass tribute ever. At Monumento a la Revolución, one of Mexico's most famous national monuments, some 13,597 people gathered to dance to his famous song 'Thriller'. It is an incredible sight to watch thousands performing the same dance moves. However, I can spot a man in Row 394 who is a little out of step. Should I alert the record authorities?

**MEXICO'S RECORD-BREAKING 'THRILLER'**

## ◢ Car Cramming

http://y2u.be/cp8xJRFirAM

Fitting as many people as possible into the classic British MINI has always been a popular record. The introduction of the updated BMW MINI gave the sport a renaissance. This all-women team crammed into the car's seats, squeezed on to the dashboard and slid into the footwells. Four more compacted themselves in the boot – creating a new record of 28. See out the clip for the heart-stopping moment when it looks like the doors won't open to let them out.

**MOST NUMBER OF PEOPLE CRAMMED INTO A MINI**

# WILD WEATHER RECORDS

Mother Nature is a prodigious record breaker and produces some of the most spectacular events you can see on YouTube. Just watch the disintegrating iceberg, dramatic twister and other gripping footage on these pages.

## Tip of the Iceberg

http://y2u.be/hC3VTgIPoGU

Over 20 million people have watched this amazing clip from the documentary *Chasing Ice*. The footage shows the historic breakup at the Ilulissat Glacier in western Greenland – the largest iceberg calving ever filmed. Glacial calving happens when an iceberg breaks off from the larger ice shelf, in this case a piece measuring 1.8 cubic miles (7.4 cubic kilometres). The Ilulissat (aka Jakobshavn) glacier produces around 10 per cent of all Greenland icebergs with around 35 billion tonnes of icebergs calving off every year.

## It's a Twister!

http://y2u.be/Q7X3fyId2U0

During the evening of 31 May 2013, the widest tornado in recorded history occurred over rural areas of central Oklahoma. It was 2.6 miles (4.2 kilometres) wide at its widest point and tracked across 16.2 miles (26 kilometres). The storm, with accompanying wind speeds of more than 295 mph (475 km/h), fortunately struck mostly in rural areas. Even so, eight people lost their lives as a result of the tornado. All of them were killed in vehicles – either they were trying to flee by outdriving the twister or they were storm chasers filming the cataclysmic event.

THE WILDEST TORNADO EVER RECORDED

RECORD-BREAKING LIGHTNING STORMS

## ▲ Everlasting Lightning

http://y2u.be/yyWkLsdJjPI

In 2014, an area of northwestern Venezuela, where the Catatumbo River meets Lake Maracaibo, was officially recognized as having the most frequent lightning storms. Known as Relámpago del Catatumbo – the Catatumbo Lightning – this "everlasting storm" appears almost every night. Averaging 28 lightning strikes per minute for up to 10 hours at a time, it can spark as many as 3,600 bolts in an hour. Although many myths surround the phenomenon, scientists claim it is just regular lightning, whose frequency can be explained by regional topography and wind patterns.

## The Hottest Place on Earth

http://y2u.be/hwQq8yRruCM

Death Valley, California, is officially the planet's hottest place. The temperature reached a record 134°F (56.7°C) on 10 July 1913. The unique geographical and geological make-up of the valley – the lowest place in America – turns it into a huge convection oven, sending temperatures past 120°F (49°C) on numerous occasions. And that's just the air. Ground temperatures often exceed 200°F (93°C) – hot enough to fry an egg (there are YouTube videos to prove it).

## The Day the Earth Fell Apart

http://y2u.be/ldsWlf2OSYQQ

In March 2011, a magnitude-9 earthquake shook northeastern Japan. It was the most powerful earthquake ever recorded to have hit Japan, and the fourth most powerful earthquake in the world since modern record-keeping began in 1900. It caused a tsunami and a nuclear plant meltdown and moved Japan's main island of Honshu eastward by 8 feet (2.4 metres). This compelling video shows what it is like to be caught in the midst of such a terrifying and devastating event.

# EXTREME SPORTS RECORDS

There's danger out there on the streets. Especially if you are mad enough to try to go faster, higher, lower than anyone else in your chosen extreme sport.

## Sacré Bleu!

http://y2u.be/8CJURZ5HAs4

French athlete Taig Khris is a hero of the inline skating world but is as well-known by the French public for skating off tall buildings. Having taken a plunge from the first floor of the Eiffel Tower in 2010, Khris now jumped from the Sacré-Coeur – the highest point in Paris. He flew down the 492-foot (150-metre) ramp, taking off with the whole city behind him, and soft-landed on an inflatable half-pipe. He set a new world distance record with a long jump of 95 feet (290 metres).

## ▶ Hopping Mad

http://y2u.be/aWs8z5UsuxY

Bunny hopping – jumping over obstacles without dismounting the bicycle – is a skill requiring control, technique and immense power. It is a staple trick of the BMX fraternity, but you won't see anything like this at your local park. The record belongs to Dutchman Rick Koekoek, one of the top riders in the world, who amazed spectators in this display at the 2014 London Street Trials Battle. Rick's insane jump could quite literally take your head off; he cleared an incredible 4.6 feet (1.43 metres).

WORLD CHAMPION BUNNY HOPPER

# Air Time

http://y2u.be/JrM4KVNwB94

BMX legend Kevin Robinson has endured over 50 concussions and 25 broken bones, but has held his record for years. On a summer's evening in Central Park with the New York city skyline as a backdrop, Kevin sped down a ramp 60 feet (18.29 metres) high at over 45 mph (72 km/h), then up a 27-foot (8.2-metre) Super Quarter Pipe to air 27 feet above the ramp – more than 50 feet (15.2 metres) in total, the highest ever BMX jump.

# ▼ Back-Breaking Work

http://y2u.be/Z-OsL4eCgP0

Records don't just happen. New Zealand's Jed Mildon not only spent three intensive months training for his historic triple BMX backflip, but he also had to build a super-ramp, 66 feet (20.12 metres) high, into a hillside in order to do it. Jed had kept his attempt to become the first ever rider to perform three full backwards rotations secret before attempting it in front of 2,000 spectators. They watched spellbound as he careered down the long ramp, shot up a 11.8-foot (3.6-metre) super-kicker, became airborne and created history.

# 100-Foot Backflip

http://y2u.be/N93aKejme5l

"I was like 'Holy moly, I forgot how long I'd be in the air,'" Daredevil Cam Zink told ESPN after his monumental 100-foot (30.48-metre) backflip in California in 2014 . "Man, I'm just staring in the sky for like ever." The daredevil hit 46 mph (74 km/h) going downhill before he took off on the world's longest dirt-to-dirt mountain bike backflip and then made a perfect landing. Cam compared his 100-foot breakthrough to the four-minute mile, expecting others to soon take the record further. We'll see …

RECORD TRIPLE BACKFLIP

# ▼ Skateboard Limbo

http://y2u.be/7HEPRZuRWvc

Like many young kids Gagan Satish, a Bangalore schoolboy, loves to get out on his rollerskates. Not many have a talent like Gagan though. He skated nearly 230 feet (70 metres) with his face just 5 inches (12.7 centimetres) from the ground – passing under 39 cars on the way! Gagan has only been rollerskating for three years, but even more incredibly, he is only six years old. Obviously his experience helped him break the record; the previous holder was only five!

CHAMPION LIMBO ROLLER SKATER

# SUPER SPORTS STARS

You don't have to be a big-time pro to be a sporting record breaker. A former NASA scientist, a teenage cheerleader and 6,000 students all wrote their name in the book in style.

## Skipping Sisters

http://y2u.be/ikRD0KbYUGw

When Rachael Dale appeared with other members of the British skipping team on the BBC children's programme *Blue Peter* she was asked to attempt to beat the world record for one minute speed skipping. In a spellbinding performance Rachael managed 332 jumps – exactly matching the existing record. The record holder was present and was sportingly cheering Rachael on – it was none other than her sister Beci (her original record-breaking skip is also uploaded on YouTube).

## ▼ University Challenge

http://y2u.be/ZdkU4oDcp40

Forget Oxford and Cambridge or Harvard and Yale; the greatest university rivalry is between the University of California in Irvine and the University of Alberta in Canada. Since 2010 the two colleges have had a running battle to seal the record for the largest dodgeball game. Alberta were the first to make a mark with 1,198 players but since then the honours have swung back and forth. In 2012, in a game involving 6,084 participants, Irvine took the title, but who knows what the Canadians have planned?

WORLD'S LARGEST DODGEBALL GAME

## Flipping Brilliant

http://y2u.be/v9hNgGnbi-Q

"I was looking at world records and I just happened to see the most consecutive back handsprings," said teenage cheerleader Mikayla Clark from Atlanta. "I was like, 'Oh, she did 36, I think I can beat that.'" Handspringing is a discipline that requires suppleness, stamina and strength and Mikayla's is no mean feat. She spent the football season training before flipping along the length of the school athletic track. In just over 30 seconds she destroys the record, racking up a total of 44 backflips.

## ▲ Putting It Right

http://y2u.be/htmbMSRj1SQ

Dave Pelz quit being a NASA scientist in 1976 to concentrate on his golf coaching. Using scientific methods he became an expert in the "short game" – shots made from within around 100 yards of the hole. In 2004, his research paid off. Filming a TV segment for the Golf Channel during PGA Championship week at Whistling Straits in Kohler, Wisconsin, Pelz holed a 206-foot (62.79-metre) putt – beating broadcaster Terry Wogan's previous record of 33 yards (30.2 metres) at Gleneagles.

### THE WORLD'S FASTEST PITCH

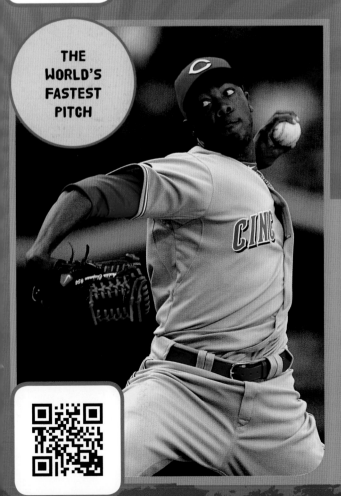

## ◄ Pitch Perfect

http://y2u.be/ngubly4hpHw

Nicknamed the Cuban Missile or the Cuban Flame Thrower, Cincinnati Reds pitcher Aroldis Chapman threw the fastest recorded pitch speed in Major League Baseball history. On 24 September 2010, against the San Diego Padres, his pitch was clocked at 105.1 mph (169.1 km/h). Pitching to the Padres, Chapman had thrown every ball at over 100 mph (169 km/h) before the monumental delivery to Tony Gwynn in the eighth inning. A year later, a Chapman pitch was recorded at 106 mph (170.6 km/h), but this was disputed by other speed devices and remains unverified.

# PURE STRENGTH

You won't see weights being lifted like this down the local gym. These guys pull, flip and lift in eye-watering feats of strength that just don't seem possible.

## Pinkie Pull-ups

http://y2u.be/AMIOAQ-TB1I

Many of us would struggle to lift even a cup of tea with our little finger, but Indian weightlifting champion Maibam Itomba Meitei has no such problem. He's been training for 14 years and has the strongest pinkies in the world. Hooking his two little fingers onto a specially designed iron bar, the 26-year-old lifted his bodyweight of 8 stone (51 kilograms) until his chin was over the bar. Then he did it again – and again, for 16 consecutive lifts in 30 seconds.

## The World on His Shoulders

http://y2u.be/BQZjC7cNbyE

In 1988 in Canberra, Australia, weightlifter Leonid Taranenko lifted the greatest weight ever – 266 kilograms (more than 586 pounds). The day before the tournament, Paul Coffa, General Secretary of Oceania Weightlifting Federation, offered Taranenko big money for a world record lift. "His mood changed instantly," said Coffa. "He went into a world of his own ... He was not interested in anything else. No one could imagine the transformation of a man who was ready to lift the biggest weight on the planet."

THE WOMAN WHOSE STRENGTH IS HER HAIR

## ▼ Down on the Farm

http://y2u.be/2BMwlRiB2jo

Mark Henry is a big figure on the American wrestling circuit. Standing 6 foot 4 inches (1.93 metres) and over 400 pounds (181 kilograms), he is the largest athlete in Olympic history and has a mouth to match. Before he was a wrestler, Henry was a champion weightlifter, setting a number of world records, and he is often referred to as the strongest man on Earth. Here he is at his best pulling a record-breaking two trucks at once with a combined weight of over 100,000 pounds (45,360 kilograms).

## Flipping Marvellous

http://y2u.be/UNHR38qJ2jk

What do muscle men do when they get old? They start breaking strength records. In 2011, Derek Boyer, 16 times a national champion and the undisputed king of Australian strongmen, was at the end of his career. No worries, mate! Boyer went along to the iconic Outback Festival in Winton, Australia and broke the world record for flipping a car 10 times. He enjoyed it so much, he went back in 2013 and beat his own record – in a flipping amazing 2 minutes, 52 seconds.

## ▼ Letting Her Hair Down

http://y2u.be/YoBFYQiOCHE

Circus of Horrors star Anastasia IV (Joanna Sawicka from Wimbledon, London) is proud of her hair. She combs it for hours and washes it five times a day. Anastasia isn't vain, she needs to do this to keep her record-breaking hair in top condition. Anastasia spends most of her stage show dangling from her hair, but also lifts record weights with her locks, lifts people, and, in this clip, pulls a 2.5-ton funeral hearse 65 feet 6 inches (20 metres) down the road in under four minutes.

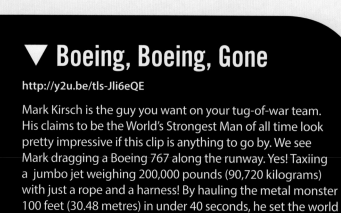

# ▼ Boeing, Boeing, Gone

http://y2u.be/tls-Jli6eQE

Mark Kirsch is the guy you want on your tug-of-war team. His claims to be the World's Strongest Man of all time look pretty impressive if this clip is anything to go by. We see Mark dragging a Boeing 767 along the runway. Yes! Taxiing a jumbo jet weighing 200,000 pounds (90,720 kilograms) with just a rope and a harness! By hauling the metal monster 100 feet (30.48 metres) in under 40 seconds, he set the world record for the heaviest ever plane pull.

THE MAN WHO DRAGGED A BOEING

# BACKWARDS RECORDS

Doing something backwards is a favourite among record breakers. Sometimes skilful, sometimes dangerous and often looking rather silly, our heroes set to their task without fear of neck ache ...

## ◀ Thunder's Back

http://y2u.be/o4fzSkAgNP4

Thunder Law of the Harlem Globetrotters must have enjoyed setting his record of longest basketball shot (see page 28). The next year he set out to break a different record – and succeeded. This time he took the shot facing away from the hoop – an incredible feat of skill and strength. His one-handed backward launch propelled the ball 82 feet, 2 inches (25.04 metres) – almost the length of the court and 10 feet (3.04 metres) further than the previous record) – for a perfect three pointer.

## Driving in Reverse

http://y2u.be/5DFz3JJY_o8

When professional golfer Rocky Bowby contracted cancer, one of the ambitions on his bucket list was to get in the record books for the longest backward golf shot. Bowby developed the backward approach first as a drill to improve his swing and then as a way to rehabilitate from back surgery. His record drive of 283 yards (258.8 metres) was against the wind (he hits just over 400 yards/365.8 metres conventionally). Just for fun, Rocky has learned to play a full round of golf backwards and beats rivals playing off a single-figure handicap.

## Keep Going Bikewards

http://y2u.be/pI5MvRtI89g

Australian Andrew Hellinga learned to ride backwards to impress the girls at school, but then put his skills to good use. In a 24-hour challenge for charity, he rode backwards for 209 miles (337 kilometres). With a unique style of sitting on top of the handlebars and facing backwards, Hellinga broke the existing 24-hour record of 112 miles (180 kilometres) in just 10 hours, 15 minutes. After a brief stop to celebrate, he carried on to nearly double the record at an average speed of over 8.6 mph (14 km/h).

## ▼ Ramping It Up

http://y2u.be/XUIiffRMfVQ

THE WORLD'S LONGEST REVERSE RAMP JUMP

Ever wondered what skateboarders do for thrills when they grow out of their baggy shorts and elbow pads? Professional skateboarder Rob Dyrdek set 21 different skateboarding records before moving on to be a TV star and all-round entertainer. He broke doughnut and banana eating records on his hit show *Rob & Big*, but once a ramp man … In the parking lot of a theme park, Dyrdek reversed his Chevrolet Sonic off one ramp and flew 89 feet 3¼ inches (27.2 metres) through the air to land cleanly on another. What a guy!

## ▶ Bowling Backwards

http://y2u.be/ex5iwpBHhdw

YouTube has opened up an opportunity for records to be broken all over the world. You no longer need officials and men in blazers to set an authentic record, just a clear video of your achievement. Step forward the most unlikely looking hero in Andrew Cowen of Illinois, USA. Andrew was determined to throw a 300 score (pretty impossible for us weekend bowlers) – while facing the wrong way. He managed 280 – two more than the official record – and might have reached his 300 if not for that second frame slip-up.

# TOTALLY GROSS!

Are you ready to be completely grossed-out? These are some of the yuckiest, flesh-creeping and nauseating clips on the site. And, of course, they are absolutely mesmerizing.

## Human Ashtray

http://y2u.be/78H5Lpx2Tyo

It might just be the most unlikely anti-smoking message ever, but you have to credit Richie Magic for trying. Magic, who is himself a heavy smoker (just listen to his voice!), puts out cigarettes with his tongue. To publicize his message, he goes for the world record and puts an astonishing 70 burning cigarettes into his mouth. Afterwards, he confesses that his tongue is black and numb, the skin inside his mouth peels away and he can't eat solid food for a few days. I'm sure it's worth it, though ...

MILK-SQUIRTING CHAMPION

## ▶ Squirt Off

http://y2u.be/H7EPI1N_aN4

It's the ultimate squirting milk from the eye battle! Please don't try this at home. It hurts and can lead to lasting damage to the eyes. Plus, it's altogether a pretty repulsive thing to do. That said, have a look at these two heroes squirting it out for the record. The trick, apparently, is to snort milk up your nose, close your mouth, block your nostrils and build up the pressure in the nose. The milk has nowhere else to go but to escape through a duct in the eyes. Yuk!

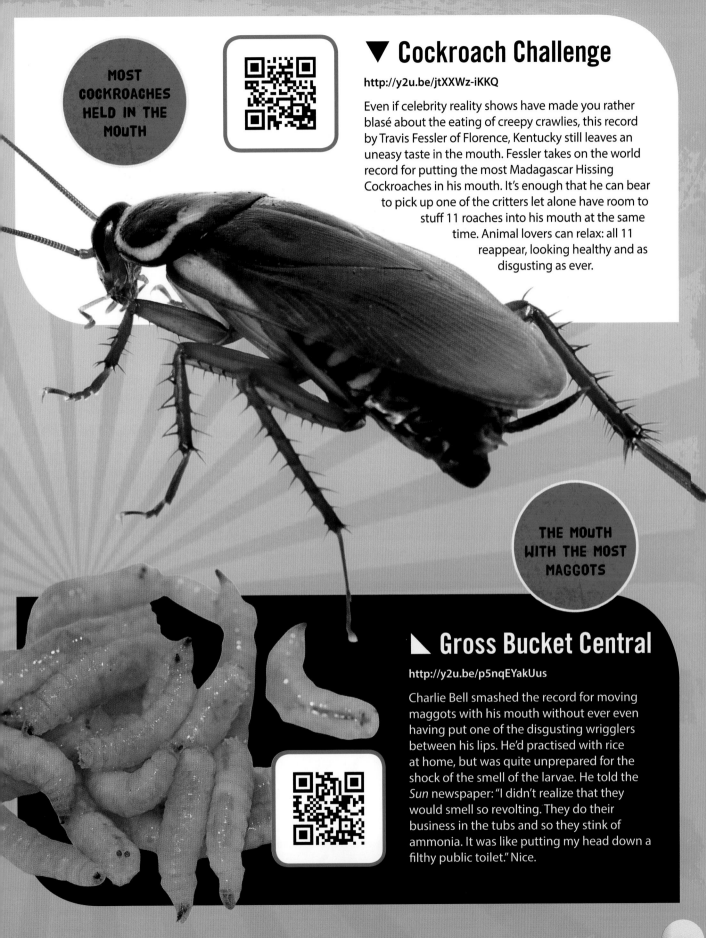

MOST COCKROACHES HELD IN THE MOUTH

## ▼ Cockroach Challenge

http://y2u.be/jtXXWz-iKKQ

Even if celebrity reality shows have made you rather blasé about the eating of creepy crawlies, this record by Travis Fessler of Florence, Kentucky still leaves an uneasy taste in the mouth. Fessler takes on the world record for putting the most Madagascar Hissing Cockroaches in his mouth. It's enough that he can bear to pick up one of the critters let alone have room to stuff 11 roaches into his mouth at the same time. Animal lovers can relax: all 11 reappear, looking healthy and as disgusting as ever.

THE MOUTH WITH THE MOST MAGGOTS

## ◤ Gross Bucket Central

http://y2u.be/p5nqEYakUus

Charlie Bell smashed the record for moving maggots with his mouth without ever even having put one of the disgusting wrigglers between his lips. He'd practised with rice at home, but was quite unprepared for the shock of the smell of the larvae. He told the *Sun* newspaper: "I didn't realize that they would smell so revolting. They do their business in the tubs and so they stink of ammonia. It was like putting my head down a filthy public toilet." Nice.

# MULTIPLE RECORD HOLDERS

For some people, breaking one mention in the record books is just not enough. One sniff of glory has them searching for more.

## Keepy-Uppy King

http://y2u.be/oFA0JLWgVGY

Until Ashrita (see below) came along, Paul Sahli proudly boasted the "most records" crown. The Swiss juggler – now a senior citizen – was a master foot juggler and still claims 64 world records. Unlike Ashrita, his records vary only in the size of the ball he's juggling. Foot juggling a football for over 14 hours; a 13-pound (3-kilogram) medicine ball for 1 hour, 6 minutes and a tennis ball while climbing up a fire ladder for 50 steps ...

## Record-Breaking Royalty

http://y2u.be/Dj7U8xcnn_0

Ashrita holds the ultimate world record: the record for holding the most records. Born Keith Furman in New York, he was inspired by his spiritual guru to undertake feats of physical endurance. He has set more than 500 official records since 1979 and holds more than 200 existing records, including Fastest Mile Balancing Milk Bottle on Head, Longest Underwater Hula Hooping, Catching Grapes in His Mouth (86 in a minute), and Balancing a Pool Cue on Finger for Largest Distance (8.95 miles/14.4 kilometres).

HOLDER OF THE MOST WORLD RECORDS

## Ahead of the Pack

http://y2u.be/UvczxVxmqMY

As his video says "Muhammad Ali is the greatest, Bolt is the fastest, Lee Riley is the fittest." Former British elite paratrooper, Riley is the first and only person ever to hold every world record for running with a 40-pound (18-kilogram) pack – at the same time! His record-breaking runs carrying the equivalent of two car tyres include the 400 metres in under a minute, a mile in five and a quarter minutes and a marathon in just over four hours.

## ▲ Houston, We Have a … Beatle

http://y2u.be/hpvE8kVGeZI

Once a member of the Beatles, Paul McCartney has gone on to become the most successful musician and composer in popular music history. He has a host of sales and radio play world records, the most Number 1 hits ever, the most frequently covered song in history ('Yesterday' has been sung by over 4,000 artists), the largest paid audience for a solo concert (350,000 people, in 1989 in Brazil) – and, perhaps best of all, he was the first artist to broadcast live to space.

# BRILLIANT BUILDINGS

Yes, it's interesting to discover the dates and dimensions of the world's record-breaking buildings, but how much better is it to watch one being built fast – or demolished in seconds? Thank you, YouTube!

## Sandcastles in the Air

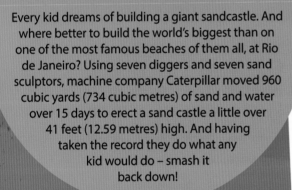

http://y2u.be/nltqM_Q-cwg

Every kid dreams of building a giant sandcastle. And where better to build the world's biggest than on one of the most famous beaches of them all, at Rio de Janeiro? Using seven diggers and seven sand sculptors, machine company Caterpillar moved 960 cubic yards (734 cubic metres) of sand and water over 15 days to erect a sand castle a little over 41 feet (12.59 metres) high. And having taken the record they do what any kid would do – smash it back down!

## ▶ Room to Swing a Cat?

http://y2u.be/NECN6tpwxCY

The Keret House is the world's narrowest home. Squeezed into a crevice between two buildings in the centre of Warsaw, it is 122 centimetres (48 inches) wide at its widest – and 72 centimetres (28 inches) at its narrowest! The triangular house has a bedroom, bathroom and kitchen with just enough space for a single inhabitant to live and work. "It requires a sense of humour, as you cannot stay long in a place like this," says the building's architect Jakub Szczesny.

WORLD'S MOST NARROW HOME

## ▶ A Tilt at the Record

http://y2u.be/UEfeqgXPHPA

Everyone has heard of the Leaning Tower of Pisa, some have heard of the leaning tower of Suurhusen (which leans a further 1.22 degrees). However, as of 2010, there is a new leaning king on the block – the Capital Gate in Abu Dhabi. In contrast to the previous record holders, the Capital Gate was intentionally designed to lean. Despite being one of the tallest buildings in the city at 35 storeys high, it keels as much as 18° westwards; more than four times that of Suurhusen.

## ▼ To Kingdom Come

http://y2u.be/oiftDBtCFt8

Seattle's Kingdome stadium was only 24 years old when it was blasted to smithereens in 2000. Once heralded as a futuristic marvel, it had grown a reputation as the ugliest stadium in America. So around 6,000 holes were drilled into the 100,000-ton structure and crammed with dynamite. At a click of a button they were exploded with detonation cords burning at 24,000 feet (7,315 metres) per second. In the space of 20 seconds the city's once great landmark was levelled to the ground in the world's fastest ever demolition.

## A Building Sight

http://y2u.be/Ps0DSihggio

There are no building workers sitting on the walls eating their lunch and shouting at passers-by in this video. They are far too busy erecting the fastest building on the planet. This time-lapse video shows the 30-storey Ark Hotel being constructed next to Dongting Lake in Hunan Province in just 15 days, or 360 hours. And this is no shoddily built edifice. All of the structure is soundproofed and thermal-insulated and the hotel is built to withstand a major earthquake.

THE FASTEST DEMOLITION IN HISTORY

# ▼ Hit the Roof

http://y2u.be/iD4qsWnjsNU

The Khalifa Tower (Burj Khalifa), a skyscraper in Dubai, is the highest man-made structure in the world. Unsurprisingly it has been a target for BASE jumpers wanting to set records. Two jumpers created a world record in 2008 when they illegally jumped from the 160th floor, but this 2014 "official" jump surpassed that. Fred Fugen and Vince Reffet leapt from a platform built above the top of the building, some 2,716 feet 6 inches (828 metres) from the ground. They actually did it six times to make sure the video was impressive!

THE
WORLD'S
TALLEST
BUILDING

# SUPER-FAST RECORDS

The best records are those feats we think we can do pretty well ourselves. Just watch these guys text, clap or throw a frisbee – and see if you might match them.

## Dressed/Undressed

http://y2u.be/ksymwAItE0M

This one is just a bit of fun. Who would think it was possible to undress in less than a second? The speedy disrober is a Japanese actor and comedian called Herachonpe. His appearance on a Japanese TV show is a feature of many YouTube compilations as he has a unique way of taking his clothes off. It's got to be a world record, surely, and at the very least, it will raise a smile.

## In the Balance

http://y2u.be/bDFZok9uzdk

Try to balance an egg. It isn't easy, they are just not made for it. It would take most people five minutes to balance one egg. Back in 2003 Bryan Spotts helped break the record of most eggs balanced at once with 1,290 eggs. But he was hungry for more records, so he invented the category of fastest time to balance a dozen eggs. Finding his record broken, Bryan decided it was time to poach it back – at a shopping mall in Hong Kong.

## ▼ Happy Clapper

http://y2u.be/ORp2nzwHXN0

His hands are almost a blur, like the wings of a hummingbird, but you can still hear the individual snaps as Bryan Bednarek claps a mighty 804 times in a minute. Bryan is a picture of zen-like concentration as he keeps up a rhythm of 13 beats a second, his palms meeting to make sure each qualifies as a clap loud enough to register on a nearby monitor. One thing is for sure ... he certainly deserves a round of applause.

RECORD-BREAKING HAND-CLAPPING

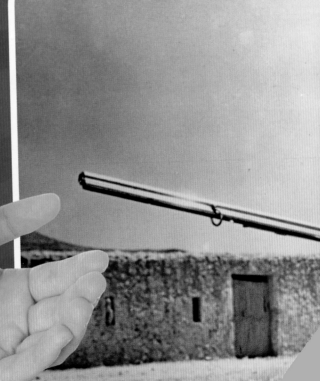

# ▶ Fstst Txtr in Wrld

http://y2u.be/87GSLXM4lko

Of course the texting record is held by a teenager. But 17-year-old Brazilian Marcel Fenandez Filho is no slacker. He's a physics student who just happens to be nifty with the fingers. Want to try? With perfect spelling and punctuation he texted: "The razor-toothed piranhas of the genera Serrasalmus and Pygocentrus are the most ferocious freshwater fish in the world. In reality they seldom attack a human." In just 18.19 seconds.

# ▲ Quick on the Draw

http://y2u.be/iS9uGktUCrY

The self-proclaimed Fastest Man with a Gun Who Ever Lived, Bob Munden went to that great shootout in the sky in 2012. He left behind a legend of a gunslinger whose records will never be beaten, and although this is clearly puffed-up myth, there is no doubt he was quick on the draw. It took him just .0175 hundredths of one second to draw his gun. In his lifetime Munden set and reset 18 world records for walk and draw; drawing shooting and holstering and for quick-fire accuracy.

# Speedy Frisbee

http://y2u.be/TO2RQj-L7gg

Simon Lizotte was a frisbee prodigy. Dubbed "The Wunderkind", Lizotte, from Bremen in Germany, has dominated the German Disc Golf scene for years. He was the 2012 European champion and is renowned in the game for his power on the drive. He holds the record for the longest disc throw (863.5 feet – 263.2 metres – the length of two-and-a-half football pitches), but here he notches up the fastest throw ever recorded at 89.5 mph (144 km/h).

**WORLD'S FASTEST GUNSLINGER**

# SOUND AND VISION

They say it takes all sorts to make a world ... but the record world has the strangest inhabitants of all. Call them weird, call them mad; they call themselves "record breakers"!

◄
## Stay Chilled

http://y2u.be/692ZbCf3BHU

Ex-Busted lead singer Charlie Simpson risked frostbite in order to break the world record for the coldest concert. Simpson played a full 15-minute set in -30°C (-86°F) temperatures in Oymyakon, Siberia. Dubbed the Pole of Cold, it is said to be the coldest village on Earth. The 27-year-old singer had to expose his fingertips in fingerless gloves in order to play his guitar and claimed to have lost the feeling in his fingers for two days after the show.

**THE COLDEST CONCERT IN HISTORY**

► ## Heard That Scream Before?

http://y2u.be/cdbYsoEasio

In a 1963 western, *The Charge at Feather River*, Private Wilhelm is shot by an arrow. His cry was added using a pained yell that was first recorded for a 1951 Gary Cooper western. The cry, now dubbed "the Wilhelm Scream", was reused in films for the next 60 years and is the most used sound effect in film history. Often a film geeks' in-joke, it appears in low-budget films as well as multi-million-dollar blockbusters such as *Star Wars* and *Toy Story*.

# Best in Belch

http://y2u.be/CsCYii7Y-ZY

The Italian crowd go mad like they've just won the World Cup. Nearly. One of their own, Elisa Cagnoni, has just recorded the loudest female burp ever. Elisa's emission clocked in at a window-rattling 107 decibels, pretty much a level reached by a blast of a car horn. She does, however, have a rival in what some claim is an "unladylike" competition. American Jodie Parks – on YouTube as Queen of the Burps – claims to have registered a 107.7 blaster.

# ▼ Go Ape!

http://y2u.be/AYaTCPbYGdk

The 2005 remake of *King Kong* won the Oscar for Best Visual Effects. With a $250 million budget, director Peter Jackson was able to bring to life the giant gorilla and other creatures using visual devices. The 2,510 special effects used surpasses the record 2,200 set by *Star Wars: Episode III – Revenge of the Sith* (2005). Many of the shots involved featured Andy Serkis as Kong. He acted out each scene in a motion-capture suit, with his performance applied to a 3-D model of the gorilla.

RECORD-
BREAKING
SPECIAL
EFFECTS

# CRAZY CRITTERS

There's no such thing as a fair fight in the wild. Clawing, biting, stinging and kicking are all allowed. These guys are the best in the business.

## ◀ Angry Bird

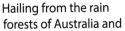

http://y2u.be/YA58sS3x2Oo

Hailing from the rain forests of Australia and New Guinea, the Cassowary has a bony crest on its head capable of knocking down small trees, and dagger-like sharp claws. Growing up to 6 feet (1.82 metres) tall and weighing in at over 130 pounds (59 kilograms), it can reach speeds of 30 mph (48 km/h) – and is capable of kicking with both legs at the same time. They have gutted dogs, slaughtered horses and have maimed and even killed humans. The most dangerous bird by far …

## Tough Guys

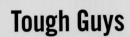

http://y2u.be/SUC0_HjNFBs

You'll never guess who wins the world's toughest creature competition. Forget lions, crocs or even cockroaches – you'll only see these hard cases through a microscope. Tardigrades are tiny creatures which look like cute swimming bears. They can live in boiling water, solid ice and nuclear fallout; they can survive a decade in a desert without a drop of water to drink, or in the deepest trenches of the sea. And now they have been revealed as the first creature to survive in space.

## ▶ Packing a Punch

http://y2u.be/ti2Uoc1RXuQ

The Mantis shrimp is a fabulous creature. A shrimp-sized lobster, it has big bug eyes, comes in dazzling colours and packs the fastest and strongest punch in the animal kingdom. Sometimes referred to as "thumb splitters", their claws are strong enough to split human appendages, and the shrimp has a punch stronger than a .22 calibre pistol. It has even been known to smash the glass of aquariums when riled. Just watch this slow-motion footage of this champion slugger throwing a right hook!

THE SHRIMP THAT PACKS A PUNCH

## ► Iron Jaws

http://y2u.be/akbpHX0Wbvw

The human bite exerts a pressure of around 120 psi (pounds per square inch). It's enough to chomp through an apple or a piece of toffee. Lions and sharks have jaws that are five times as strong – good for tearing raw flesh apart or ripping through a small boat. But the iron jaws of the animal world belong to the Nile Crocodile. These beasts can snap at 2,500 psi (and have reached 6,000 psi), twice as much again as the feared shark.

## ▼ Highly Poisonous

http://y2u.be/UETfZLsWWAM

The Inland Taipan – or the Fierce Snake, as it is sometimes known – is the most poisonous snake on the planet. It lives in the dry areas of Australia and feeds on small mammals, its venom being especially adapted to kill them effectively. It is an extremely fast and agile snake, which can strike with extreme accuracy and almost always releases venom. One drop of its poison can kill around 100 full-grown men in as little as 30–45 minutes if left untreated.

**THE WORLD'S MOST DEADLY SNAKE**

69

# AMANZING FOOD RECORDS

Groceries – they're not just for eating, you know. You can use them in art, construction, as a pastime – and to break records. Here's some food for thought ...

## ▶ Pumpkin Pride

http://y2u.be/8eQljtg3tAA

This was the moment the pumpkin world had been waiting for: the first ever one-ton pumpkin, earning farmer Ron Wallace a $10,000 prize. The historical event happened in 2012 at the All New England Giant Pumpkin Weigh-Off when Wallace's colossal pumpkin was lifted onto the scale by a forklift truck. It topped out at an astounding 2,009 pounds (911 kilograms), beating the record set just the previous day by 165 pounds (75 kilograms) to become the largest fruit ever grown.

## Use Your Noodle

http://y2u.be/E0Zntlya904

As celebrity chef Gordon Ramsay discovers, hand pulling noodles is more difficult than it looks. In his television series in 2008 he went head-to-head with Shanghai-born, London chef Fei Wang. Unfortunately he was up against a master who had spent 10 years perfecting his art in China. Stretching, folding and twisting repeatedly, Fei Wang transforms the lump of dough into a cats' cradle of noodle strands just millimetres thick. Enough to fill a record eight bowls of noodles in the allotted three minutes.

THE INCREDIBLE ONE-TON PUMPKIN

## ◀ Coffee Break

http://y2u.be/Kng_LuXl6HI

Albanian artist Saimir Strati's previous work includes a portrait of Leonardo Da Vinci with nails, a galloping horse with toothpicks and singer Michael Jackson with paint brushes. This time he made a mosaic – the largest in the world – with a million coffee beans. Strati says he wants his image of a Brazilian dancer, a Japanese drummer, an American country music singer, a European accordionist and an African drummer to spread the message of "One world, one family, over a cup of coffee."

## ▼ Spaghetti Junction

http://y2u.be/v7SgBUq6_qk

Spaghetti Bridge competitions are held in universities around the world as a test for students' knowledge of engineering, physics and design. The bridges are made of only spaghetti and glue and are tested for how much weight they can sustain before they shatter. The Budapest Technical University has a great reputation for setting records and it was their students Miklós Vincze and Csaba Jaró who created Hoverla 5. A beautiful and, as it proved, historic construction, it finally collapsed under a weight of 1,257 pounds (570.3 kilograms).

RECORD-BREAKING SPAGHETTI

# SUPER STRENGTH RECORDS

How desperate can you be to get your name in the record books? These record breakers seem to feel no pain as they take one or more of their senses to the limit.

## ▼ Smashing Breasts

http://y2u.be/cTuNCuDNH4g

American Susan Sykes, better known by her stage name, Busty Heart, has an unusual profession: she uses her size 34M breasts to crush objects. She has officially been acknowledged as having the world's strongest breasts. She can crush 34 cans with her chest in just one minute. Here she appears on *Greece Has Talent* (she made the semi-final of *Germany's Got Talent*, but received a unaminous "No" on the US version) showing off that skill and smashing a baseball bat as an bonus.

## Bring a Lump to the Throat

http://y2u.be/5PJrYAU2uBE

It is time to really take heed of those "don't try this at home" warnings – this guy is putting his neck on the line – quite literally. Professional strongman Mike "The Machine" Bruce is renowned for his tough-guy feats, especially those demonstrating his neck strength – he even hung himself and withstood the strain! In this clip he sets a world record by having seven .625-inch (1.5-centimetre) steel bars bent across the front of his throat in less than 60 seconds.

THE RECORD-CRUSHING BREASTS

## ▶ A Nose-Blowing Champ

http://y2u.be/6LGiq717r9Q

23-year-old Jemal Tkeshelashvili is capable of inflating hot water bottles to the point of bursting – with his nose! These rubber bottles require ten times more air pressure to inflate than a party balloon, so Jemal needs great lung capacity and the ability to push the air out of his nostrils with incredible force. Here, in 2009 in his home town of Tblisi, Georgia, he blew up and exploded three hot water bottles in 23 seconds, including one being sat on by a hefty adult.

**THE MAN WITH A CHAMPION NOSE**

## Tongue Tied

http://y2u.be/tnwI4d6AsUk

Thomas Blackthorne is a quality circus sideshow act with world records that will bring tears to your eyes. To earn the record for the World's Heaviest Weight Lifted by Tongue, Thomas inserts a hook into a piercing through his tongue (which is already pretty gross!). He then hooks onto a large fish tank-sized box full of pasta weighing 27.5 pounds (12.5 kilograms) and lifts it with his tongue. See if you can bear to watch it all of the way through!

## Coconut Shy

http://y2u.be/FMj48Lxc9GM

When Jeffrey Lippold broke a world record 21 coconuts with his elbows on a US TV show, it seemed a pretty impressive effort (you can see it on YouTube). So it is quite difficult to take in the performance of taekwondo master Edin Kajević from Bosnia in November 2014. The accuracy of his blows is unerring and the power immense as he obliterates 40 of them. He even runs out of coconuts to smash as his coach scuttles around trying to find more targets for his sledgehammer elbows.

## ▼ There's No Yolk

http://y2u.be/wyCB0OVCnA8

Canadian Darryl Learie's 100 or so records, many of which you can view on YouTube, vary from Fastest Slideshow on YouTube to Largest Collection of Personal Videos, but the majority are based around his push-up ability. This attempt finds Darryl performing his routine by placing one hand on a raw egg and the other behind his back. A combination of the egg's unique construction, Darryl's ability to withstand pain and his great physical fitness enables him to complete a record number of push-ups without breaking the egg.

# HOLDING OUT FOR A HERO

This awesome selection illustrates just how wide-ranging the record-breaking heroes are. Some rely on physical endurance, others on know-how and some just collect crazy stuff!

## ◀ Rubik with a Twist

http://youtu.be/Iw4xJpvJ4AE

Rubik's Cube solving records are usually not the most impressive feats to watch. They stare at the cube for a minute, furrow their brows, twist the sides a few times and it's done. North American Speed Cube Champion Anthony Brooks obviously agreed, so he took the Rubik's challenge a step further. He went for Most Cubes Solved Underwater in One Breath, needing to twist five of the cubes to perfection in order to set the record.

## ▶ Hair Today ...

http://youtu.be/NvILbEoUu0c

John Reznikoff's most prized possession is a frame containing a couple of strands of black hair. They were taken from Abraham Lincoln on his deathbed, and he estimates they are worth $500,000. Reznikoff has the largest collection of celebrity hair in the world, including locks from King Charles I; Neil Armstrong, first man on the moon; Marilyn Monroe; and even the singed locks of Michael Jackson. If *Jurassic Park*-style DNA "reincarnations" ever become reality, John could have some interesting dinner parties ...

**THE MOST VALUABLE COLLECTION OF HAIR**

# ▼ Micro Motor

http://youtu.be/6GBwWodOls0

This clip tells the story of British inventor Perry Watkins's attempt to build the world's smallest legally roadworthy car. Using the bodywork of a children's toy car and the chassis and engine of a quad bike, Watkins engineered a hilarious-looking vehicle that was 41 inches (104 centimetres) high, 26 inches (66 centimetres) wide and 52 inches (132 centimetres) long and capable of 37 mph (60 km/h). Just about squeezing into the driver's seat, he was able to take it for a spin – even if he did have to ignore the laughter of other drivers.

THE WORLD'S SMALLEST CAR ON THE ROAD

# ▼ Gym Hero

http://youtu.be/LzciOAhto78

The Plank is a favourite exercise for the gym bunnies. With muscles rippling they lie horizontally, supported only by their forearms and toes. Some even manage to hold the position for a minute or two. So, here's Chinese police officer Mao Weidong in 2014. A member of the SWAT team fighting organized crime, Weidong held the excruciating position for four hours, 26 minutes, more than an hour past the previous record. He only stopped as it matched his wife's birthday on 26 April. A tough man and a romantic too!

THE LONGEST PLANK EVER HELD

# TOTALLY DIFFERENT

The record breaker can never stop to ask why. Thankfully these record setters never questioned putting themselves in harm's way, playing a silly instrument or building a huge chocolate train …

## Soap Star

http://y2u.be/eyuPwChQxDU

Canadian bubble artist Fan Yang is a record-setting expert with 18 bubble-based records to his name. His shows feature any number of amazing soapy bubble feats, but his huge people-containing bubble is the showstopper. At a show in Vancouver, Canada, he constructed a bubble 164 feet (50 metres) long and 13 feet (4 metres) high in which he enclosed a record 181 people. Yang claims to have invented a seven-ingredient recipe for bubble formula, but vows to keep the ingredients a family secret.

## ▼ Choco Choo Choo

http://y2u.be/Fd2pW0SjWLY

The highlight of Brussels Week of Chocolate in 2012 was a creation by Maltese master chocolatier Andrew Farrugia. His chocolate train was 111.7 feet (34.05 metres) long and was made of 2,833 pounds (1,285 kilograms) of chocolate. Officially the World's Largest Chocolate Structure it had a locomotive and seven wagons, modelled on different-era Belgian train coaches and included one with a bar and restaurant. Big enough for the most dedicated chocoholic, it contained over six million calories!

RECORD-BREAKING CHOCOLATE SCULPTURE

## ◀ Action Hero

http://y2u.be/gS_YQrDmHp4

Hong Kong actor Jackie Chan has appeared in over 150 films, many of them martial arts movies and thrillers. He began his career as a stuntman for the legendary Bruce Lee but continued to perform his own stunts even when he became a star. In the process he has fractured his skull and broken many of the bones in his body. He finds it impossible to get insurance, but is compensated with the record of having performed the Most Stunts by a Living Actor.

**WORLD CHAMPION STUNT PERFORMER**

## ▶ Take a Bow – or Two

http://youtu.be/mPni3__sWus

Perhaps no one pointed out to Ukrainian musician Oleksandr Bozhyk that when a piece of music says it is a concerto for four violins, that does not mean they all have to be played by the same person. At a live concert in Lviv, Ukraine in 2012, the vituoso violinist took up two bows and four violins and proceeded to play – pretty well considering – the soundtrack from the film *Requiem for a Dream*. It was, of course, the most violins ever played by one person at the same time.

**THE MOST VIOLINS IN ONE GO**

# COOL CAT RECORDS

There is plenty of kitten action and a lot of celebrity cats on YouTube, but not many make the record books. Here's a select few who are on the road to purr-fection.

## The Miserable Moggie

http://youtu.be/l4A9ji851Rc

Colonel Meow was the first superstar cat of the social media age. When he died in January 2014, he was mourned by millions around the world. A Himalayan-Persian crossbreed, the Colonel was loved for his grumpy scowl and his followers on Facebook and Instagram revered him as an adorably fearsome dictator and prodigious Scotch drinker. He is remembered in a number of YouTube videos but also for holding a world record for the longest fur (an average of 9 inches/ 22.9 centimetres).

## Pricey Kitty

http://youtu.be/rZEgvh_u_Ts

The Ashera is the millionaire's cat of choice. Said to be a crossbreed of two exotic wild species – the African Serval and the Asian Leopard cat, with a dash of domestic cat – the Ashera cat was touted as the world's newest, rarest, and largest breed. DNA tests have led to claims that they are actually pure Savannah cats, but what is unquestionable is that they are the world's most expensive moggie. Only five are "created" each year and some fetch as much as $125,000.

## ▶ The Pocket-Sized Pussy

http://y2u.be/1vdVRuqQUb4

Singapura are nicknamed Velcro Cats because of their, sometimes irritating, desire to stay close to their owners. They have been acknowledged as the smallest breed of cat in the world. The full-grown males only reach around 7 pounds (3.1 kilograms), while females can weigh a paltry 4 pounds (1.8 kilograms, about five large cans of cat food). Some claim they were originally river or "drain" cats in Singapore, while others have suggested they were a cross between Abyssinian and Burmese breeds.

THE WORLD'S SMALLEST CAT

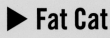
# ▶ Fat Cat

http://youtu.be/7dVn7KNP0co

Garfield is one of the great cartoon cats, right up there with Tom, Top Cat and Sylvester. Now, there is a real-life Garfield, who shared some of his animated namesake's gargantuan appetite and indolence. Garfield was brought to an animal rescue in Long Island, New York, after his owner passed away and he shocked the volunteers with his obesity. He tipped the scales at 40 pounds (18 kilograms) – an average cat weighs around 10 pounds (4.5 kilograms) – and earned the distinction of being the fattest cat in the world.

**THE WORLD'S FATTEST CAT**

# ◢ Big Big Cat

http://youtu.be/xBznm54nVMM

There are cats, big cats and then there are Ligers.  Ligers are the offspring of a male lion and a tigress – huge animals which do not exist in the wild and are only bred in captivity. Hercules, who usually lives at the Myrtle Beach Safari wildlife preserve in South Carolina, is the biggest of them all. He is 6 feet (1.82 metres) tall, 12 feet (3.65 metres) long and weighs 900 pounds (408 kilograms) – as big as his parents combined. He may look a handful, but his keepers say he's a real pussycat.

**THE WORLD'S LARGEST LIGER**

# CRAZY CROWD RECORDS

Whoever said, "Three's a crowd" wasn't in the record-breaking business. To register in the record books you need great organization, silly costumes and people in their thousands ...

## The Largest Gathering on Earth

http://y2u.be/3a3F_XcBJQg

The Hindu pilgrimage Kumbh Mela is the largest human gathering on earth for the same cause on a single day. It is held every three years and alternates between Nasik, Allahabad, Ujjain and Haridwar. The celebration at the Holy Sangam in Allahabad, last held in 2013, is the largest and holiest of them all with around 100 million people attending to bathe in the Sangam – the confluence of the holy rivers Ganga, Yamuna and the mythical Saraswati.

## ▼ Horde of the Dance

http://y2u.be/wiU-n_IWAio

Dubliners crowded along the banks of the city's Liffey River to watch the successful attempt on the longest ever continuous line dance. The 1,693 dancers from 44 different countries, all tutored in the Riverdance steps, stretched from the Samuel Beckett Bridge to the Sean O'Casey Bridge. On the signal from an Irish Navy ship, New Yorker Jean Butler, the lead dancer in the first ever show of Riverdance in 1994, led the massed dancers for over five minutes to gain the record.

THE WORLD'S LONGEST LINE DANCE

## ◀ Red Head Rampage

http://y2u.be/Rt7mCsZnlcw

Gingers, auburns, strawberry blondes – hundreds of them. All in one place! Since 2005 all manner of gold tops have been meeting at the Roodharigendag (Redhead Days) Festival. The festival has been growing every year with naturally ginger-haired people from more than 80 countries assembling in a park in Breda in the Netherlands. They claim up to 5,000 attend the festival's events, and their record is for redheads in the same place for 10 minutes, which stands at 1,672 in 2013.

## ▶ Flying the Flag

http://y2u.be/ENetD1cWSsE

India's rivalry with Pakistan is often hostile, but in December 2014, the stakes were raised when India stole the world record for the largest human flag from their neighbours. Over 50,000 volunteers began gathering at 5.00am in the YMCA ground in Chennai, but it wasn't until noon that they were in position to form the tri-colour flag. Pakistan's previous record was just short of 29,000 – they've probably already started working on recapturing the title.

## ▼ Ever So Elfish

http://y2u.be/lu8dsjoW5-o

Nearly two thousand Santa's little helpers, aged between nine and 15, put on red, green and white hats, matching T-shirts and pointy plastic elf ears, and formed up outside a shopping mall in Bangkok. Those participating were required to stand still for 10 minutes with their elf ears and hats on. Some didn't make it and others were disqualified for not putting on their elf ears, but 1,792 correctly attired and standing still were enough to set a new record.

RECORD-BREAKING NUMBER OF ELVES

# RECORD-BREAKING DOGS

It's dog beat dog in the competition for canine records. You'll love these proud pooches as they show off their record-breaking skills.

PEANUT

THE UGLIEST DOG IN THE WORLD

## ◀ Ugly Mutt

http://youtu.be/7AkYSGllKTk

Two-year-old Peanut, a mutt who is suspected of being a Chihuahua/Shitzu mix, doesn't have a lot going for him. He was seriously burned as a puppy and lived in an animal shelter for nine months before he found a home. On the looks side he has matted hair, protruding teeth and looks as much rodent as canine. However, in California in 2014, Peanut found fame. In a hotly contested competition, he swept the floor with the other hideous hounds and was crowned the World's Ugliest Dog.

## A Two-Legged Friend

http://y2u.be/5CaDC-ou7kg

His Facebook page has over 14 million likes, he has over 850,000 followers on Instagram and he numbers pop princess Katy Perry amongst his friends. Jiff the pint-sized Pomeranian from Los Angeles has got to be the most famous dog in the world. Of course it helps that he is as cute as a button, especially when dressed up, but Jiff is also a talented pooch: he is the world's fastest dog on both his hind legs and on his front legs.

## Puppy Love

http://y2u.be/t_Q9c_r5MuY

It was the wedding of the year, a lavish $200,000 ceremony organized by a celebrity wedding planner. The bride wore a spectacular gown valued at $6,000, while the groom was attired in a designer tuxedo. For this was the most expensive pet wedding in history – a charity event that saw Baby Hope, a Coton de Tulear puppy, marry Chilly Pasternak, a Poodle. The event was even officiated by a celebrity pet in Triumph, the Insult Comic Dog, well-known on American TV.

THE WORLD'S SMALLEST DOG

THE CHAMPION SURFING DOG

## ▲ Surf's Pup

http://youtu.be/FJqS2vZMakI

Abbie Girl, an Australian Kelpie, is a rescue dog with a rags to riches story. Needing rehabilitation for trauma, Abbie Girl was taken to the beach by her new owner, Michael Uy, in order to develop her self-confidence. She immediately took to surfing, on boogie boards and long boards. Soon she became the world's greatest surfing dog, riding breaks nearly 6 feet (1.82 metres) high and setting the record for the longest wave surfed by a dog – 65 yards (59 metres).

## ▲ Pocket-Sized Pooch

http://youtu.be/fTEIdAyYkac

Like many dogs Heaven Sent Brandy, the Chihuahua from Florida, USA is not allowed on the furniture. In her case, it's just because if she jumps off, she'd break a bone. Measuring just 6 inches (15.2 centimetres) from tail to nose, the adorable four-year-old is no bigger than a can of cola and is the world's smallest dog in terms of length. She's a nervous little creature – but who can blame her, when every hulking great human in sight wants to cuddle her?

# ENDURING PASSION

Breaking records can require years of grooming; hundreds of hours of practice; meticulous arrangement or serious organization skills. And some just happen in an instance of pure chance.

## ▶ Record Nailed

http://youtu.be/sD8N3HVvmFs

Christine Walton hasn't cut her fingernails for over 20 years. Known as the Duchess, Christine is a rock singer who also happens to have the longest fingernails in the world. A mother of six girls and grandmother of three, she has a combined length of over 20 feet (6 metres) of nails on both hands. The Duchess insists that having such extensive nails doesn't stop her living a normal life, claiming she can cook, clean, drive and wash with ease. However, she admits using her knuckles to text!

## ▼ Domino Effect

http://y2u.be/_1x99bOX7Yo

Patrick Sinner was only 12 years old when he vowed to break a domino world record. It took three years and 10 attempts, but eventually he was as good as his word. Along with his friends, Patrick from Keferod, Germany, created a colourful spiral 26 feet (7.92 metres) in diameter made up of an incredible 30,000 multi-coloured dominoes. They spent 40 hours putting it together and checking each section worked effectively, before toppling their first domino. Nine minutes later, he had done it: the world's largest spiral of dominoes.

THE LONGEST
FINGERNAILS
IN THE WORLD

# Hoop Dreams

http://y2u.be/NiQaDgj8Z10

Record holder Jin Linlin got her first hula hoop when she was 13. Fast forward 10 years and she has broken her own world record three times. "I never imagined making a career out of this ... I just liked it," she said. In 2007 she set her first record by simultaneously spinning 105 hula hoops and went on to break her own feat, twice, spinning 262 hoops. In 2011, the petite champion struggled to lift her 305 hoops, but still managed to spin them to glorious effect.

THE LARGEST GATHERING OF WALLYS

## ▲ Where's Wally

http://y2u.be/Chnui_Jqxb8

In best-selling book *Where's Wally?* (known as *Where's Waldo?* in America and often given other names around the world) readers have to find the character dressed in a red and white shirt and hat and black-rimmed spectacles. You won't have any difficulty finding him in this clip. Over 3,500 adults, children and even dogs turned out in Merrion Square in Dublin dressed in Wally outfits. They managed to set a new world record for number of people dressed as the popular children's literary character.

## Heads Up

http://y2u.be/n0sGeCHnB0o

In 2011, Norwegian soccer club Odd Grenland Skien were leading Tromsoe IL 2-1 in a Norwegian Premier League match. As the game reached its conclusion, Tromsoe won a corner. Desperate for an equalizer they sent their goalkeeper into their rivals' area. When play unfolded, things didn't quite go to plan. Instead it resulted in the longest-range headed goal ever, Jone Samuelsen's effort from 187 feet (57 metres) launching him from obscurity to internet sensation. In 2014, Samuelsen would make his debut for the Norwegian international team.

# AMAZING ATHLETES

Every sport has its record breakers. These stars from lesser celebrated sports, including Lacrosse, Table Tennis, Ice Skating and CrossFit, have some pretty amazing achievements to crow about ...

## Hot Shot

http://y2u.be/SyUD21inENA

Lacrosse is often referred to as "the fastest game on two feet". The rubber ball is propelled at astonishing speeds when passed between players and even faster in shots on goal. Mike Sawyer of the Charlotte Hounds is one of the legends of the modern game. He has broken goalies' helmets with his shots, so it was no big surprise when he stepped up at the 2013 Major Lacross League All-Star Game Fastest Shot Contest and flung this 114 mph (183 km/h) humdinger goalwards.

## ▼ To Me ... to You ... to Me ...

http://y2u.be/p9XkigqHIBg

Mima Ita was a Japanese table tennis prodigy. When just 10 years old, she became the youngest person to win a match at the Japanese senior table tennis championships. Here she is – still only 11 – on the set of the fabulously titled Japanese TV show *100 Handsome Men and Beautiful Women* hitting the ball with metronomic precision 180 times across the table – The Most Table Tennis Counter Hits Ever. Now in her teens, Ita has embarked on an already successful table tennis career.

YOUNGEST TABLE TENNIS CHAMPION

# ► A Woman's Whirl

http://y2u.be/VYV5jq1oMm0

It's enough to make the viewer feel giddy, but twirling Russian ice skater Natalia Kanounnikova says she is immune to it. "I don't really get dizzy. From spinning so often, I have kind of built up a resistance to it." Natalia spun her way to a world record of 304.47 revolutions per minute on the reality TV show *Skating's Next Star*. Despite her amazing spinning aptitude, Natalia's other skating attributes are apparently not at a standard to win her any gold medals.

# ▼ Jump at the Chance

http://y2u.be/kPZvtlDLjpl

This is an unofficial world record, but there appears no reason to doubt it – and it is exceptional. It features Kevin Bania, a CrossFit athlete (CrossFit is a sport featuring weightlifting, sprinting and jumping exercises). Bania attempts a record standing box jump which involves jumping onto a box or level surface. From a standing start, he leaps from the floor to a platform 5 feet 4.5 inches high (1.63 metres). Bania himself stands 5 feet 10 inches tall, so he is within six inches (15 centimetres) of jumping his own height.

THE MAN WHO JUMPS ALMOST AS HIGH AS HIMSELF

# WILD SPORTS

Terrified by the high board at the swimming pool? Dizzy on the top storey of the multi-storey car park? Then perhaps you should just sit down and watch some who know no fear ...

## ▼ New Ball Game

http://y2u.be/NehU-6NCBco

Zorbing is the sport of rolling down a hill in the kind of plastic sphere given to bored hamsters. Protected by a pocket of air between them and the edges of the ball, the participants can thrust the ball forward but have limited control over the direction. Miguel Ferrero from Spain, nicknamed "the adventurer", was encased in a Zorb ball and threw himself down a ski run at La Molina in the Pyrenees. He reached a record speed of 31.2mph (50.2km/h).

THE FASTEST ZORBING ON RECORD

## ◄ Extreme Swimming

http://y2u.be/IJY8VgmvXHc

Diane Nyad became the first person to swim the 100 miles (160 kilometres) from Cuba to Florida without a protective shark cage. Braving rough seas, the fear of shark attack, vomiting from salt water intake and wearing a heavy suit to withstand jellyfish stings, Diane succeeded on her fifth attempt over 35 years – her fourth since turning 60.

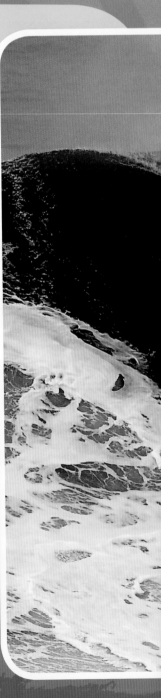

# Fjord Focus

http://y2u.be/u7MerWuCYfw

Slacklining is like tightrope walking but scarier. The rope is not pulled tight, so it is more likely to sway and bounce as you walk. It is the ultimate test of balance. Christian Schou set the record for the highest slackline by walking across a giant rubber band 1 kilometre (3,280 feet, about four football pitches) above a Norwegian fjord. Unfortunately he forgot to register his feat. It was only after Aleksander Mork repeated the trick the following year that Schou's effort was belatedly recognized.

# ▼ Surf's Up and Up

http://y2u.be/dtVQJCq2cCM

Surfing legend Garrett McNamara caught a towering 100ft wave off the coast of Nazare in Portugal. Risking being slammed into a reef or the ocean floor, he beat his own record by 1 foot (30 centimetres). That too was set off Nazare where an underwater canyon generates some of the world's biggest waves. "You are just going so fast," McNamara told ABC Television. "And you're just chattering, flying down this bumpy, bumpy mountain. Your brain is getting rattled. Your whole body is getting rattled."

THE LARGEST WAVE EVER SURFED

# TRULY REMARKABLE

It's a wonderful record-breaking world and YouTube contributors across the globe are out filming every remarkable event and achievement.

## Octomum

http://youtu.be/04g4HPdQWZU

Nadya Suleman has patented the name "Octomum". It is just one of many ways she has attempted to earn the money to look after her family. She has 14 children including the eight born together – the most babies delivered at a single birth to survive. Having given birth to the Octoplets in January 2009, Nadya has rarely been out of the media since. She has been criticized for the fertility treatment, for taking inappropriate employment and for claiming welfare benefits – but continues to care for the children.

## ▼ Pop-Up Painting

http://youtu.be/RwtWZd-sbMc

In June 2014, world-famous Chinese artist Yang Yongchun unveiled a special piece of art. Named *Rhythms of Youth*, it depicted the impressive architectural landscape of Nanjing and the Yangtze River that runs through it. Not only was it the largest and longest street painting in the world, measuring an astonishing 1,200 feet (365 metres) long and covering 28,000 sq. feet (2,600 sq. metres), but it was also an anamorphic painting – created in a distorted manner to make it appear three-dimensional.

THE LONGEST STREET PAINTING

## ▲ Sting in the Tale

http://y2u.be/jHFZ60WqX-E

Thailand's Kanchana Kaetkaew has earned her right to be calledthe Scorpion Queen. In 2002, she spent a world record 32 days in a room with 3,400 live scorpions. Six years later she prepared to break the record by a further day, this time with 5,000 scorpions. Before she went into the glass enclosure, she gave the audience a special treat. She held a venomous scorpion in her mouth for 2 minutes, 3 seconds – which in itself was a record.

THE RECORD FOR LIVING WITH SCORPIONS

## ▼ Water Colours

http://y2u.be/OZwAbQ8iv_A

Jesper Kikkenborg is a Danish marine biologist and artist. Combining both his fields of expertise he produced a painting at the Blue Planet Aquarium in Denmark. This was no ordinary painting – Kikkenborg wore scuba diving gear and painted his picture inside the four million litre Ocean Tank. Named *Mother Ocean*, it featured eagle rays, hammerhead sharks and other exotic fish. It took him 23 hours over nine days and measures 48 feet square (4.5 metres square) – the largest underwater painting ever.

## Escape to Victory

http://y2u.be/nYz8-ZnTdIo

Magician Louis Yan, Hong Kong's answer to David Copperfield, frees himself from a straitjacket and chains under water in less than 26 seconds at a shopping mall's New Year countdown celebration in Hong Kong. He is in plain view throughout the escape, so it is mind-boggling how he manages to free himself in such a short time. All he reveals is that it had been the result of three months' practice. Yan also features on YouTube giving the world's largest ever magic trick.

93

THE
HIGHEST
EVER LEGO
TOWER

## ▼ Tower Power

http://y2u.be/KuQkUmz9fmY

They might make film heroes now, but for years Lego bricks were purely for construction. Thankfully, some are still preserving the art of the interlocking brick. In the shadow of St Stephen's Basilica in Budapest, children, locals and Danish engineers constructed the highest ever Lego tower. Rising 114 feet (34.76 metres), the towering spire was made of 450,000 colourful bricks and appropriately topped with another great toy – the Rubik's Cube, a puzzle designed by a Hungarian professor of architecture Ernő Rubik.

# IT TAKES ALL SORTS

Isn't it a wonderful record-breaking world when a twerking champion and a fast food toy collector can share a page with one of the greatest footballers ever?

## ▼ Hard Twerk

http://youtu.be/otZmEyIDGsY

After Miley Cyrus's twerking at the 2013 MTV Video Music Awards, New Orleans rapper Big Freedia set about reclaiming the dance. The self-proclaimed Queen of Bounce claimed twerking had been started by the "bounce" dance scene of New Orleans. So, in her home town, Big Freedia – the stage name of Freddie Ross – cued her hit 'Duffy', and led a world record 410 dancers, ranging from age 8 to 80, as they shook their rumps for two continuous minutes.

CHAMPION TWERKING IN NEW ORLEANS

## Shoe Business

http://youtu.be/3mmaCGZHtuQ

The trainer store at your local shopping centre might have a good range of shoes but nothing compared to Jordan Michael Geller's ShoeZeum in Las Vegas. Geller holds the record for the world's largest collection of sneakers. He had more than 2,500 pairs, all but eight of which were Nikes (and included one of every model of Air Jordans ever made). Sadly, the ShoeZeum is now closed, and Geller has sold most of his collection, but we still have the YouTube clip to remember his epic venture.

## Want Fries with That?

http://youtu.be/IX4aXsiSjSE

Mike Fountaine loves a McDonalds Happy Meal. Mike started working for the burger chain in 1968 at 15 years old and received a lapel pin to start his collection. Now he owns virtually every Happy Meal toy the burger chain has ever produced. And that's not all. Nine rooms in his house in Pennysylvania, USA, house a collection of over 1,000 McDonald's cups and 11,700 lapel pins as well as uniforms, buttons displays and a life-sized Ronald McDonald.

## ▶ Clean Sweep

http://y2u.be/TWJap_smAxY

No one in football can match the honours won by German Franz Beckenbauer. As an elegant defender in the 1960s and 70s he won five German League titles and three European Cups (now Champions League) as well as lifting the World Cup and European Championship as captain of West Germany. Then, as a manager, he won the French title with Marseille, the German title with Bayern Munich and the World Cup with West Germany (one of only two men ever). Some record!

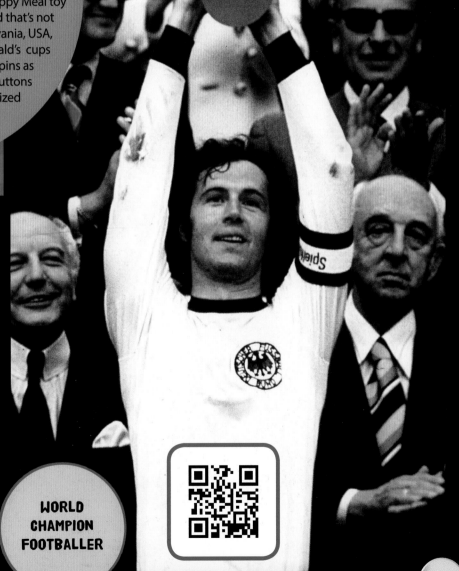

WORLD CHAMPION FOOTBALLER

# ▼ Pulling Faces

http://y2u.be/72NW0pobAnw

Tang Shuquan of Chengdu City, China spends a lot of time hoping the wind doesn't change direction and he stays like that. Named the King of Deformed Faces, Tang spent 10 years working on being able to contort his face into the ugliest shapes possible. After winning the world record for gurning, Tang, who has the extraordinary ability of biting his own nose, even challenged all comers – offering a £10,000 prize to anyone who can match his face-stretching skills.

THE GuRNING WORLD CHAMPION

# MAD MOVIE RECORDS

Roll the credits! From Bollywood to Hollywood, the glamorous and exciting world of the movies lists the famous and the not so famous in its annals of achievement.

**AN EXPENSIVE RECORD BREAKER**

## ◀ Titanic Record

http://youtu.be/zCy5WQ9S4c0

The 1997 film *Titanic* staring Leonardo DiCaprio and Kate Winslet was, at that time, the most expensive film ever made. It was worth it. *Titanic* became the most successful film ever in terms of box office and critical success. It has the most Oscar nominations (14, tied with *All About Eve*) and the most Oscar Awards (11, tied with *Ben Hur*) and is the second-highest-grossing film ever (*Avatar* is first) having taken over two million dollars at the box office.

## Devil in the Detail

http://youtu.be/4MMBdQ6pSV4

Based on the true story of a pair of man-eating lions who preyed on railway workers in Kenya, *Bwana Devil* was a pretty poor 1950s B-movie following the fashion of jungle adventure films. However, the film was a box office smash and set a trend that revived a flagging industry in the 1950s. For *Bwana Devil* was the first 3D movie, its posters offering "A LION in your lap! A LOVER in your arms!" The whole film has been uploaded on YouTube, but it's comically atrocious.

THE MOST RETWEETED MESSAGE EVER

## ▲ Selfie Aggrandizement

http://youtu.be/GsSWj51uGnl

This was the picture that appeared on millions of phones and tablets after Ellen DeGeneres posted it on Twitter during the Eighty-Sixth Annual Academy Awards in 2014. The most re-tweeted message ever (over three million times to date)  the selfie featured Hollywood stars Jared Leto, Jennifer Lawrence, Channing Tatum, Meryl Streep, Julia Roberts, Kevin Spacey, Brad Pitt, Lupita Nyong'o, Angelina Jolie, Peter Nyong'o Jr. and Bradley Cooper, who took the photo. Ellen's comment on the tweet read: "If only Bradley's arm was longer. Best photo ever. #oscars"

## Extra Special

http://youtu.be/977TwLYyn3Q

Acclaimed director Richard Attenborough faced a real challenge when filming *Gandhi* on location in India in 1980. He was determined to re-create the great man's life as accurately as possible and had to film a funeral scene in which a million people had lined the route. Attenborough chose to film on the thirty-third anniversary of Gandhi's funeral and managed to recruit around 300,000 volunteers and actors – the most extras ever to appear in a feature film.

## Child's Play

http://youtu.be/lfP7gQzxlVQ

Most seven-year-olds are happy watching cartoons or pretending to be spacemen. Not Saugat Bista. After acting in commercials and a feature film, this young boy from Nepal decided to swap places and direct his own film. *Love You Baba*, a family drama about a father and a daughter, was well received and earned Bista the record of being the World's Youngest Director. This trailer for the film shows him at work, looking for all the world as if he had spent a lifetime studying Scorsese and Spielberg.

# TRANSPORT RECORDS

This collection of the bizarre, brilliant, marvellous and downright silly means of transport would get some strange looks down the high street.

## Lawnmower Mover

http://y2u.be/nF18um9VGp8

Next time you complain about mowing your scrubby 10-foot (3-metre) patch of grass, consider investing in a Honda Mean Mower. With a custom-made Cobra sports seat, a six-speed gear system and a fibreglass cutter deck, Honda claim their machine is the world's fastest mower. It is capable of speeds up to 130 mph (210 km/h). Piers Ward of the BBC's *Top Gear* magazine took the grass-cutting speedster for a burn-up in Tarragona, Spain and managed 116.57 mph (187.60 km/h) – it was, indeed, a lawnmower land speed record!

## ▼ Lavvy Savvy

http://y2u.be/FACWhm_8lmY

When you got to go, you've got to go – quickly! No one knows that more than plumber Colin Furze, from Lincolnshire. Luckily Colin is also an engineer and an inventor, so he was able to build the world's fastest toilet. With a powerful 140cc motorbike engine hidden under the seat, Furze smashed the previous record of 42.25 mph (68 km/h) with his 55 mph (88.5 km/h) lightning loo. See Furze's YouTube channel for other record breakers, including a mobility scooter and a pram.

THE WORLD'S FASTEST LAVATORY

# The Milkman Delivers

http://y2u.be/1BmX4ip0808

Imagine this monster bombing down your road at the break of dawn as the milkman dishes out the pints! With a few alterations the milky's electric-powered vehicle, which would usually trundle down the street at a top speed of around 4 mph (7 km/h), was turned into a speed machine. The souped-up float has BMW wheels, a chrome spoiler, four roof-mounted spotlights and a chunky front bull bar. However, it is the V8 engine which does the damage, enabling rally driver Rob Gill to hit a record-breaking 84.5 mph (136 km/h).

# Trolley Dash

http://y2u.be/Bu_qYLIU2a8

This is one shopping trolley without a wonky wheel. Matt McKeown's souped-up supermarket cart hit just short of 72 mph (116 km/h) in a trial at Elvington Airfield in north Yorkshire in 2013. McKeown set a record by using a modified Chinook helicopter starter engine, a 250cc Honda engine and an afterburner to power his shopping trolley. He confessed that above 60 mph (96 km/h) it became scarily unsteady despite being stabilized with go-kart wheels, and he is now turning his attention to a motorized wheelbarrow.

THE FASTEST HOT TuB ON FOUR WHEELS

# ▲ Car Pool

http://y2u.be/XoGKG8-9URw

What's the most unlikely thing to put on four fast wheels? How about a hot tub? Phil Weicker and Duncan Forster bought a 1969 Cadillac Coupe DeVille for $800 and over six years transformed it into a fully functioning mobile hot tub, which even bubbles as they motor along. They took their "CarPool DeVille" to the famous speed-testing Bonneville Salt Flats and despite a flooded course (nothing to do with them!), still managed to record a top speed of 50 mph (80 km/h).

# BIZARRE PEOPLE

The say: "If you've got it, flaunt it." None of these record breakers seems to have any problem flaunting their special features. And, as you will discover, they are pretty special ...

## ▼ Leg Work

http://y2u.be/JQnY9e9PLT0

The sports coach at George Mason High in Virginia can regale her pupils with her experiences as a top Russian basketball player. But you suspect they might be more impressed with another area in which she excels. For Svetlana Pankratova has the world's longest female legs. Her pins stretch 4 feet 4 inches (1.32 metres), more than two-thirds of her total height of 6 foot 5 inches (1.96 metres). On the video she is in London with the then world's shortest man – who came up to her knees!

THE WOMAN WITH THE LONGEST LEGS

## ◀ A Good Stretch

http://y2u.be/CFiGkTJt5GE

Gary "Stretch" Turner suffers from Ehlers-Danlos syndrome, a rare genetic disorder that has weakened his skin. This means he can stretch his skin away from his body to an amazing world-record-setting 6.25 inches (15.9 cm). He's put it to good use as a "strange" performer: he can make a skin tray from his stomach, big enough to carry three pints of beer, and is also able to pull the skin from his neck completely over his lower jaw.

## ▶ What a Waist

http://y2u.be/SCl7BIoA17Y

Cathie Jung first wore a corset at her wedding in 1969. She and her husband liked the look and now she is the corset queen – wearing the constrictive garment 24 hours a day. Her devotion to corsetry has enabled Cathie to reduce her waist to a record-breaking 15 inches (38 centimetres) – about the size of a jar of mayonnaise. It is an achievement even more remarkable when you consider her bust and hips are a pretty average 39 inches (99 centimetres).

## By a Nose

http://y2u.be/sINHIWI0NsE

Mehmet Ozyurek of Artvin, Turkey has been acknowledged as having the longest nose on a living person. His massive conk measures 3.46 inches (8.8 cm) long from the bridge to the tip. Compare that to the average-sized male nose of around 2.25 inches (5.8 centimetres) and you'll realize he's carrying round a fair old hooter. Mehmet carries his with pride and so he should: Romans considered the big nose to be a sign of power while Chinese associate it with wealth.

THE WOMAN WITH THE SMALLEST WAIST

# EXTREME EATING

The world of competitive eating is not for the faint-hearted or for those brought up not to shovel down their food. But it is pretty amazing ...

## Grim Reaper

http://y2u.be/3zhym9oUSGU

The "Carolina Reaper", a crossbreed between a Ghost chilli pepper and a Red Habanero pepper, has been rated as the world's hottest chilli pepper. It averages a 1,569,300 on the Scoville scale, which makes it over 900 times hotter than Tabasco sauce. There are enough chilli-eating videos on YouTube to show what excruciating results can occur, but despite that the Danish TV host, Bubber, is foolish enough to step up to the challenge. With inevitable consequences ...

## The Grape Man

http://y2u.be/BmdoO53-BoI

Steve "The Grape Man" Spalding discovered his skill when his college roommates began throwing sweets around the room. Steve amazed his friends by catching everything thrown at him – in his mouth! Over the following 15 years he practised and honed his skills and concentrated on catching grapes. He is now the proud possessor of a host of records, including catching 116 in 3 minutes and 1,203 in 30 minutes. It's not clear whether he eats them all, though ...

## ▼ Where's the Beef?

http://y2u.be/tuqPL6X-aCc

Molly Schuyler is a woman in the male-dominated world of speed eating. A mother of four, Molly is of less-than-average build (under 10 stone/63.5 kilograms) but she has a prodigious talent for eating. She often takes on and beats the big names in competitive eating and in 2014 broke the world record for eating a 72-ounce (2-kilogram) steak. Molly scoffs the plate-sized piece of meat in less than three minutes (halving the previous record) and reportedly had a burger an hour later as she was still hungry!

**WORLD RECORD MEAT EATER**

## ▶ Kobayashi – the Master Eater

http://y2u.be/P1GBf0ioYKI

Kobayashi is arguably the world's greatest competitive eater. He has been blowing away his rivals in competitions for 15 years. He has pigged down hot dogs, tacos, satay, noodles and even cow brains in world record time. Here is the master in action on a TV show in 2012 in which he set the record for most Twinkies eaten in a minute. A Twinkie is a Golden Sponge Cake with Creamy Filling. One is delightful. Two can be sickly. Kobayashi ate 14 ...

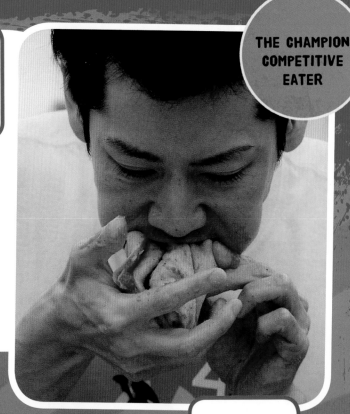

THE CHAMPION COMPETITIVE EATER

## ▼ Blowing Bubbles

http://y2u.be/alBUeRNOalw

Champion bubble blower Chad Fell of Alabama blew a bubblegum bubble with a diameter of 20 inches (50.8 cm) which remained intact for a full five seconds. It was no fluke. Chad takes his skill seriously. He gets through two bags of Dubble Bubble a week in practice and know his science. He drinks cold water to regulate the temperature in his mouth and chews for 15 minutes to cut down the sugar to aid elasticity before carefully adding air.

## Hungry Fella

http://y2u.be/zfYhaqNAF70

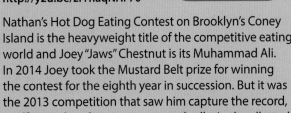

Nathan's Hot Dog Eating Contest on Brooklyn's Coney Island is the heavyweight title of the competitive eating world and Joey "Jaws" Chestnut is its Muhammad Ali. In 2014 Joey took the Mustard Belt prize for winning the contest for the eighth year in succession. But it was the 2013 competition that saw him capture the record, scoffing 69 hot dogs – sausage and roll – in the allotted 12 minutes. Joey is also a world record holder in eating deep-fried asparagus, pork ribs, matzoh balls and hard-boiled eggs.

## Egg-ceptional

http://y2u.be/uCgok8lmVol

Not only does speed-eating heroine Sonya Thomas rank among the best in her field, she also has the best nicknames. She sometimes goes under the fantastic moniker "The Leader of the Four Horsemen of the Esophagus". More often she is known as "The Black Widow" in recognition of the eight-stone petite woman's ability to out-eat men four times her size. As wells as the feat seen here, Sonya holds a number of other records, not least consuming nearly five pounds of fruitcake in 10 minutes.

107

## ▼ Furious – and Tearful

http://y2u.be/Jky1gDSw0AM

Furious Pete (real name Pete Czerwinski) is a major player in the competitive eating world. He holds six world records, including polishing off 17 bananas in two minutes, wolfing down 15 hamburgers in 10 minutes, guzzling a bottle of olive oil (25 fluid ounces/750 millilitres) in 60 seconds, and tucking away 17 Jaffa Cakes in 60 seconds. Pete confesses, however, that eating a whole onion in 43 seconds was the toughest of all. Watch his first failed attempt, and you'll see why.

**MULTIPLE FOOD EATING WORLD RECORD HOLDER**

# NICE MOVES!

These entertaining clips pay homage to the hot-footers who have danced themselves into a pirouetting, head-spinning, pole-leaping, tip-tapping, mascot jiving, record-breaking world.

## Spinning Queen

http://y2u.be/_bT756ywafU

Since she was 10, Sophia Maria Lucia has been America's darling. The young ballerina appeared on hit TV shows such as *Dancing with the Stars*, *America's Got Talent* and *The Ellen DeGeneres Show*. The dance prodigy has her own dancewear line and even a book. There is no denying the girl has talent and now she has a new nickname, "The Spinning Queen". In this clip, filmed in 2013, Sophia performs an amazing world record 55 consecutive pirouettes.

## ▼ Body Popping

http://y2u.be/yHzpcBuQlpM

Julia Gunthel goes by the stage name Zlata. A 27-year-old Russian living in Germany, she is also known as the Most Flexible Woman on Earth. Watching the way she twists and bends her body around, it is hard to imagine that Julia actually has a spine. Her balloon bursting act just has to be seen to be believed. She manages to burst three balloons in 12 seconds, using the curve of her back as a press. That just can't be comfortable.

## ▶ Human Propeller

https://youtu.be/EZfVAxG2-h4

The headspin, a staple power move of breakdancing, is a routine where the dancer's body is rotated while standing on his head. Just watch the poise and strength of 23-year-old Aichi Ono of Japan as it seems he tries to screw his head into the ground. The Human Tornado, or Spinboy as he is also called, spins at a breakneck speed, racking up an incredible 142 rotations in a minute on a TV show in Japan.

RECORD-BREAKING NUMBER OF HEADSPINS

## Turn on the Tap

http://youtu.be/KUyfBhmGZGI

Anthony Morigerato is a tap dancer, choreographer and teacher and is a legend in the tap dancing world. Renowned for his awesome performances, he also holds the world record for the fastest tap dance ever. The dance is tested by recording the tap sounds (rather than steps) over 60 seconds. At Eleanor's School of Dance in Albany, USA, Anthony tapped out a simply amazing 1,163 steps – that's nearly 20 taps a second! This clip shows the master tapper in action ...

## Pole Dance

http://y2u.be/k60aeDbB_vw

The Cheraw Dance, involving dancers stepping in and out between a pair of horizontal bamboo poles, is a skilful and mesmeric folk dance. As part of the Chapchar Kut, a harvest festival in Mizoram in northeast India, more than 11,900 dancers in traditional costumes gathered to perform the dance. Using 6,710 bamboo sticks and dancing on a football field and three kilometres of road, they set a new world record as the "largest and longest bamboo dance".

# THAT'S GOTTA HURT!

"Now that has got to hurt." Sometimes you feel as of you are about to experience the pain yourself as you watch these record breakers undergo self-torture. Of course you aren't. Still, Ouch!

## Doing His Nut

http://y2u.be/mkgDDCMKXXc

Next Christmas, when you are wrestling with a pair of nutcrackers and a walnut that won't crack, think back to this clip. It is from the Punjab Youth Festival in Lahore, Pakistan in 2014. Here, martial arts expert Mohammad Rashid sets about cracking 155 walnuts in only a minute – using his head. This man is deadly with his own nut, leaving just a wake of broken shells as he heads around the table at breakneck speed.

## ▼ Nice and Icy

http://y2u.be/b-Mr1RV3Qxc

Stig Severinsen has a lung capacity of 470 fluid ounces (14 litres) – more than twice the average man's – which enabled him to hold his breath underwater for a world record 22 minutes. More impressively, Stig, in just Speedos and a mask, slipped through a hole in a frozen lake in east Greenland and swam 250 feet (76.2 metres) under the ice. "I'm not different from any other person," Stig told *Men's Journal* magazine. "I just have the ability to shut down the sensory register for pain and discomfort." Of course, hardly different at all.

## The Marriage Bed

http://y2u.be/WXPyKqW2vn8

Here's record-breaking strongman Jon Bruney allowing his wife, Amy, in on one of his records. All she needs to do is skip rope on a board for a minute. Simple. Except under that board is a bed of nails and under that lies husband Jon. He says he grunts as he contracts his muscles to bear the weight and it sometimes puts Amy off. For the record attempt he prepared her by saying, "No matter what you hear – or hear snap – do not stop jumping, no matter what!"

# ▶ Just Buzzing

http://youtu.be/7_0LRHpbWIM

There's no sting in this tale. Ruan Liangming, a Chinese beekeeper, sat with the top half of his body covered in bees for 53 minutes, 34 seconds, smashing his own previous record of 20 minutes. Covered with a layer of honey, he sat on a stool without any protection for his eyes, nose or mouth while helpers layered approximately 100,000 bees onto his head and torso. Ruan claims keeping perfectly still minimizes the stings and that, after 19 years as a beekeeper, he is immune to their venom.

MOST TIME SPENT COVERED IN BEES

# ▲ Heavy Metal

http://y2u.be/Rj7vKStJmtA

A living confusion of tattoo and glistening metal, Elaine Davidson is the world's most pierced woman. A Brazilian-born nurse, living in Edinburgh, Elaine has 462 studs and rings (192 on her face), which saw her crowned the world's most pierced woman in 2000. But Elaine didn't stop there – as of March 2012 she had amassed over 9,000 piercings. She never removes the rings and studs, which means she carries around an extra 6.6 pounds (3 kilograms). But you wouldn't miss her in a crowd!

THE WOMAN WITH THE MOST PIERCINGS

# THE MOST EXPENSIVE

You'll be surprised at some of the things that turn up in the "most expensive" basket in the YouTube supermarket. Who would expect a second-hand car or a flashy pair of trainers?

## Fancy Footwear

https://www.youtube.com/watch?v=bMsW9t46ml8

Those trainers you've got your eye on might look expensive but they're small change compared to the $2 million shoes that *America's Got Talent* host Nick Cannon wore for the series finale in 2014. Cannon had asked Beverly Hills jeweller Jason Arasheben to make him "the most expensive shoes in the world". Jason came good with a pair of diamond-enhanced Tom Ford shoes that had more than 14,000 full-cut round white diamonds set onto white gold, with a total of 340 carats.

## ▼ $50 million for a Used Car?

http://y2u.be/n2j8ElGBzTU

Only 39 of the beautiful 1962–64 Ferrari 250 GTO cars were ever produced. Originally intended to race at Le Mans and similar events, they were soon superseded and in the 1970s fetched as little as $10,000. Now only the super-rich can afford them – if they can find one for sale. No one seems sure of how many exist, but currently the 250 holds the record for most expensive sale at auction ($32 million) and most expensive ever ($52 million in a private sale).

THE MOST EXPENSIVE SECOND-HAND CAR

## ◀ Sting in the Tale

http://y2u.be/RCcY0n_7DDs

The list of the most expensive liquids on earth is fascinating. Perfume, champagne , human blood are predictably all on the list; there are some surprises like maple syrup and nasal spray; and no computer user will be surprised to see printer ink near the top at around $8,000 a gallon. Just be thankful, then, that you don't need too much scorpion venom (used in anti-cancer drugs). Scorpions are difficult and dangerous to obtain and milk (see the video!) and their venom fetches an amazing $40 million a gallon.

## Wallet-Melting Ice Cream

http://y2u.be/PpnujjnP1Eg

It looks a pretty tasty chocolate ice cream – and at $25,000 so it should! The world's most expensive dessert, Frrrozen Haute Chocolate is available at New York's famous Serendipity 3 restaurant. They need advance notice of two weeks because this is not just a slushy frozen mix of cocoas and milk. The dessert contains more than five grams of 24-carat gold and the finest ingredients are flown in from around the globe including a garnish of La Madeline au Truffe, the most expensive chocolate in the world.

## ◀ Price Tag Player

http://y2u.be/ia-zi5oLa_0

A combination of super skills, burning ambition and a fiery personality have made Zlatan Ibrahimović the most expensive footballer ever. The combined €171.1 million spent on the sublime Swedish striker includes the €16m Juventus spent bringing him from Ajax; the €24.8m Inter paid Juve; the €69.5m Barcelona forked up for a short spell in Spain; the €24m it cost AC Milan to bring him back; and the €20m Paris Saint Germain bought him for in 2012. He's now aged 33, so could he still garner one more fee to add to the record?

THE MOST EXPENSIVE FOOTBALL PLAYER

# A LONG WAY DOWN

Some people just have no respect for the laws of gravity. It might have kept sensible folk's feet on the ground for centuries, but not your adrenaline-junkie record breaker ...

## The Birdman of Norway

http://y2u.be/ER1PGYe9UZA

Is it a bird? Is it a plane? No. It's Espen Fadnes, the World's Fastest Flying Human Being. In his flying squirrel suit, Norwegian Espen routinely leaps off buildings, bridges, mountains and cliffs – and flies. Winning a base-jumping competition in 2010, he officially became the fastest flying human. Just watch as he calmly (although to be fair he admits he's completely terrified) steps off a 4,068-foot (1,240-metre) cliff in Stryn, Norway and flies through the air at speeds of over 150 mph (250 km/h).

## Jump de Triomphe

http://y2u.be/MLejkyXbJlc

Australian motorcycle stunt rider Robbie Maddison likes a New Year's Eve party; his record-breaking end-of-year stunts have become a tradition for the thrill seeker. Few of them can beat the 2008 effort when the 27-year-old sped his bike off a 35-foot (10-metre) high ramp to the top of the 96-foot (30-metre) high replica of the Arc de Triomphe in Las Vegas. Having set the world record for the highest motorcycle jump, he then plunged the 80-foot (24-metre) drop back – breaking his hand in the process.

## ▼ Look Mum, Just Hands!

http://y2u.be/Wy3SuhEQHVg

Dan Osman was the fastest bare-handed speed climber in the world. In this ascent, he climbs Bears Reach, a 400-foot (122-metre) rock face of Lover's Leap in California in just 4 minutes, 25 seconds. He uses no ropes or grips, just gaining hold with his feet and his bare hands. Osman held other mountain stunt world records, including a freefall rope jump of 1,100 feet (335 metres) at the Leaning Tower in Yosemite, California. Sadly, this was also the spot where he met his death after a tragic rope malfunction.

THE FASTEST BARE-HAND CLIMBER

# The Sky's No Limit

http://y2u.be/FQSvowsAUkl

Felix Baumgartner may have been the first and most famous skydiver to break the sound barrier, but his 2012 record lasted little more than two years. In 2014 Alan Eustace, a senior vice president at Google, fell from more than 25 miles (40 kilometres) above New Mexico, smashing Baumgartner's record. In a custom-made pressurized spacesuit, he jumped from 135,890 feet (41,419 metres), reaching a speed of 822 mph (1,322 km/h). It is claimed his body set off a sonic boom that could be heard by the recovery team on the ground.

**THE HIGHEST FREEFALL JUMP RECORD**

# Snow Business

http://y2u.be/MqlFOrSqfpg

Anders Backe is a professional skier who is no stranger to daredevil challenges. He is a top performer in slopestyle – tricks and jumps on skis – but took on the backwards challenge with gusto. Skiing down the slopes in his hometown of Vikersund in Norway backwards, he reached a preposterous 79.97 mph (128.7 km/h). "It was super fast," said Backe after setting a new world record. "I could barely hang on to my skis."

119

# COOL CONSTRUCTIONS

The world of engineering deserves a special mention in the record-breaking hall of fame. The world's greatest tunnels and bridges are spectacular examples of human achievement.

## ▶ Bridge of Size

http://y2u.be/WP1rZrB9SZI

Opened in 2009, the Sidu River Bridge in Hubei Province of China is the highest bridge in the world. It is a suspension bridge that hangs a vertiginous 1,600 feet (496 metres) above the river gorge. It spans just over 5,000 feet (1,5124 metres) across the river valley; far enough that builders had to use a rocket to string the first pilot line. Some claim it is also the only bridge in the world high enough for a person to reach terminal velocity if they were to jump off.

THE WORLD'S HIGHEST BRIDGE

## ◀ Light Fantastic

http://y2u.be/9ugUDYcr9hw

The Bund Sightseeing Tunnel is one of Shanghai's Top 5 tourist attractions and it's also the World's Longest Multicoloured Light Tunnel. Taking just five minutes to travel the 2,123 feet (647 metres) under the Huang Pu River in Shanghai, passengers travel in automated cars and experience a psychedelic trip from space to the core of the Earth and back again. Some find the journey, full of dazzling lights, strange visual effects and otherworldly voices, "mind-bending" while others have deemed it "tacky". See what you think ...

## ▲ At the End of the Rainbow

http://y2u.be/wxLnoNKSIZQ

The Banpo Bridge Rainbow Fountain is the world's longest bridge fountain. Spanning the Han River in the centre of Seoul, South Korea, the bridge has around 10,000 nozzles that shoot nearly 190 tons of water a minute. During the day, the fountain produces a hundred different displays meant to evoke waving willow branches and willow leaves. At night, 200 LED lights illuminate the fountain as it sends up dancing, rainbow-coloured jets of water in the air in synchronization with music.

## Light at the End of the Tunnel

http://y2u.be/w3TqHyalKBs

Set to open in 2016, the Gotthard Base Tunnel under the Swiss Alps will be the longest tunnel in the world. Taking a decade to build, the tunnel cuts 35 miles (57 kilometres) through the immense Gotthard Massif, and will significantly shrink the rail journey across central Europe. The tunnel has claimed the lives of eight workers as they blasted and bored through 13 million cubic metres of rock in hot and humid conditions sometimes reaching 8,000 feet (2.43 kilometres) below the surface of the Earth.

## ▼ Cliffhanger

http://y2u.be/GzJnOrr5RUE

Located in the Taihang Mountains of China, the Guoliang Tunnel is deemed the World's Most Dangerous Tunnel. In 1972, inhabitants of the village of Guoliang dug a tunnel 3,937 feet (1,200 metres) long through the rocky cliff. When opened to traffic it was soon dubbed "the road that does not tolerate any mistakes". A tight squeeze for even one vehicle, it twists and turns past 30 or so "windows", which provide views off the precipice to a tumbling abyss hundreds of feet below.

THE MOST DANGEROUS TUNNEL

# WILD RECORD BREAKERS

Another scan of the great achievers of the wild world brings forth the slow-motion sloth, the aggressive ant, the super-sized squid and a few and far-between feline.

THE WORLD'S SLOWEST ANIMAL

## ▼ Beware of the Bull

http://y2u.be/vU_thoOeQw0

The bulldog ant – also called a Bull Ant or Jumper Ant – is the hard case of the insect world. The World's Most Dangerous Ant, it is built for fighting. It measures a whopping 0.59–1.4 inches (15–36 millimetres) in length, has long mandibles and a venomous sting that inflicts death on other insects and great pain to larger creatures. But what gives them the edge is their fearlessness. They don't take kindly to visitors and will take on anything that comes near, even snakes and humans.

## ▲ Sloth Motion

http://y2u.be/OTp8W251aiQ

The three-toed sloth doesn't do anything in a hurry. It likes to sleep for around 10 hours a day, come down from its tree once a week to do its business and occasionally have a (slow) swim. These are the World's Slowest Mammals, averaging a distance of only 0.15 miles (0.24 kilometres) an hour, with a top speed of 6.5 feet (1.98 metres) a minute. They are so slow that algae grow on them. They do, however, have a good excuse; their long claws, ideal for tree life, make walking particularly uncomfortable.

# ▶ Monster Squid

http://y2u.be/xDcsByYGzSE

Armed with giant tentacles, swivelling hooks, and the world's largest eyes, the colossal squid is the largest invertebrate on the planet. Rarely seen and even more rarely caught, they live in the deep, cold waters of Antarctica. The largest of the species to be caught was a squid 30 feet (10 metres) long, caught by a fishing boat off Antarctica in 2007. The 990-pound (450-kilogram) monster, whose calamari rings would be as thick as car tyres, was immediately frozen and transported to New Zealand. This clip shows what happened when it thawed ...

THE WORLD'S
LARGEST
INVERTEBRATE

# ◀ Lesser Spotted Leopard

http://y2u.be/OUO2K_qoucE

According to the World Wildlife Fund, the Amur Leopard is probably the rarest and most endangered big cat in the world. Found along the border areas between eastern Russia and northeast China, it suffers from road building, logging and forest fires destroying its natural habitat and is also poached for its beautiful, spotted fur. With global attention the last few years have seen the wild Amur Leopard population rise from 30 to 45; the next most endangered mammal is the Javan Rhinoceros, which numbers between 50 and 60.

# SPECTACULAR SCIENCE

Making new discoveries and inventions and exploring deeper and further than ever is the business of the scientist. So it is no surprise that they set some pretty incredible records.

## Wonderstuff

http://y2u.be/WFacA6OwCjA

Graphene is a thin layer of pure carbon; it is a single, tightly packed layer of carbon atoms that are bonded together in a hexagonal honeycomb lattice. It is the thinnest, lightest and toughest material known to man as well as being the best conductor of heat and electricity. Recent scientific breakthroughs in its production have led to predictions that it will soon be used in everything from bullet-proof clothing to fold-up televisions and phones and even invisibility cloaks.

## ▼ Goodbye Moon

http://y2u.be/TU6QzMltdZA

Only 12 men have even taken a step on the moon. Only three years after Neil Armstrong's first great step, Eugene Cernan prepared to climb back to Apollo 17 as the last man on the moon. While there, Cernan set the Land Speed Record in the Lunar Rover, 11.2 mph (18.0 km/h), and spent a longer time than anyone else on the lunar surface. "When I pulled up the ladder," he says. "I knew I wasn't going to be coming this way again."

THE LUNAR SURFACE LAND SPEED RECORD

## ▼ A Galaxy Far, Far Away

http://y2u.be/7mBOQ3KrbjE

This photograph, assembled by combining 10 years of NASA Hubble Space Telescope recording, represents Man's Farthest Ever View of the Universe. By collecting faint light at the centre of the Hubble Ultra Deep Field – just one ten-billionth the brightness apparent to the human eye – NASA built a picture of a distant patch of sky. From over 13 billion light years away, it reveals thousands of galaxies, from spirals that are Milky Way-lookalikes, to hazy reddish blobs that are the result of galaxy collisions.

**THE FURTHEST VIEW OF OUR UNIVERSE**

**THE LONGEST ECHO EVER RECORDED**

## Echo ... echo ... ech ... ec ... e

http://y2u.be/VZwVl4Fvl1k

A tip-off sent Professor Trevor Cox to a huge disused oil storage tank in the Highlands of Scotland, where he recorded the longest echo ever discovered. His colleague shot a pistol with blanks down the 80-year-old tank which was twice the length of a football pitch, designed to hold 25.5 million litres of fuel, and with walls 17.7 inches (45 centimetres) thick. Professor Cox measured the resulting echo and concluded that the gun-shot resonated for a full 112 seconds. (For comparison, St Paul's Cathedral has a 9.2-second echo.)

# UNLIKELY CELEBRITIES

The millions of YouTube viewers can create the most unlikely celebrity record breakers. Among the surprising super-achievers are a scooting dog and a bunch of dancing hardened criminals.

## ▼ Exercise Yard

http://y2u.be/vsG1_eee9fg

The Philippines prisoners' dance to 'Thriller' was a YouTube hit and is still worth viewing, but this full body, resistance workout by prison inmates in Peru broke their world record for the most people dancing in a prison. The colourful display was the result of three months' practice by around 1,200 prisoners at the overcrowded Lurigancho prison in Lima. The workout saw the prisoners – many of them murderers, drug barons and other serious offenders – strutting their stuff to the sounds of the beats of reggaeton and merengue.

MOST PRISONERS DANCING EVER

# Amazing Afro

http://youtu.be/65-He8_sb_k

Fourteen years ago, inspired by an old photo of her mother sporting an afro hairstyle, Aevin Dugas from Louisiana, USA, swapped her straight locks for her own natural round style. Now she sports the world's largest natural afro, measuring 4 feet 4 inches (1.32 metres) around and 7 inches (17cm) tall. It takes two days to wash and dry her afro and she sometimes struggles to see out from it, but she does admit it makes for a really comfortable pillow.

# ▼ Dog on Wheels

hhttp://y2u.be/qKYryJ_1poQ

He's a three-year-old French Sheepdog with a special talent. Ever since he was a puppy, Norman has been climbing on board a scooter and propelling himself along. Norman balances himself on the scooter with his two front paws on the handle and a back paw on the scooter. He uses his other hind paw to push himself forward. Having already earned the moniker "Norman the Scooter Dog", he then scooted 100 metres in just over 20 seconds – a world record for a dog on a scooter!

# ▲ Power Play

http://y2u.be/sB6SwPHPEtQ

China's Three Gorges Dam was said to be the largest building project in China's history since the Great Wall. It cost $59 billion and took 15 years to construct. It is 1.3 miles (2 kilometres) wide, over 600 feet (183 metres) high, and has a reservoir that stretches 405 square miles (1.049 square kilometres). The hydropower station's 32 main turbines generated a world record 98.8 billion kilowatt-hours (kwh) of electricity in 2014, as much electricity as 18 nuclear power stations.

THE CANINE SCOOTER CHAMPION

# WORLD OF WONDER

Movie star George Clooney famously said, "I go on YouTube when somebody says to look something up." I wonder if he found any of these fabulous clips?

## ▲ Carpet World

http://youtu.be/JeEqpKr1vFg

Each year during the Holy Week preceding Easter, "sawdust carpets" line the city streets in Guatemala. Made of fine brightly coloured sawdust with dried fruit, flowers and bread, they create an incredible street art of varying and often intricate design. In Guatemala City in April, 2014 the longest ever sawdust carpet was laid. Using an estimated 54 tons of dyed sawdust , it measured 6,600 feet (2,012 metres) long – but in days was trampled away by religious processions .

## ▼ Who You Calling a Dummy?

http://youtu.be/EmkUGEirTE8

If you are the kind of person who gets spooked by ventriloquist dummies, this clip could make you feel a little uneasy. It contains wonderfully creepy footage of the dolls on display at the Vent Haven museum in Kentucky, USA. With over 800 objects in the museum, they have the largest collection of ventriloquist dolls in the world – from a figure that was fashioned by a Second World War German POW to Dolly, a dummy crafted in 2009, complete with diamond sparkling teeth.

THE LARGEST COLLECTION OF DUMMIES

# ▼ On the Bright Side

http://y2u.be/IdbKSYY38eY

It is a beautiful sight to watch the thousands of sky lanterns illuminating the evening sky of Iloilo city in the Philippines. In an amazing world record, 15,185 of the rice paper and bamboo lanterns were released into the skies above the football field of University of the Philippines. The organizer explained that flying sky lanterns was a traditional form of prayer and by cultivating inner peace they were seeking to attain world peace. There's not too much success on that front, but it does make for a magical atmosphere.

**RECORD-BREAKING RELEASE OF LANTERNS**

## ◄ Hogwarts Heaven

http://youtu.be/7cVeFUY9rPY

We may not be seeing Harry, Hermione and Ron in any more magical adventures, but in Mexico there remains a Hogwarts Heaven where they all live on. Lawyer (yes, a grown man!) Silva Vargas has spent 15 years building up his collection and owns over 3,000 pieces of Harry Potter merchandise – the biggest Harry Potter-themed collection in the world. His two-roomed hoard contains everything from magic wands to toy figurines, Gryffindor scarves and replica Quidditch brooms.

## ▼ It's All Relative

http://youtu.be/T19U-48WgRs

Sect leader Ziona Chana has 39 wives – all sharing a 100-room mansion in a holy village in India. The largest family in the world lists 32 sons, 18 daughters, 22 grandsons, 26 granddaughters and seven great-grandchildren all living under one roof. While the youngest wife gets the bedroom next to Ziona, the eldest wife runs the household and organizes the meals, which can see them preparing 30 chickens, peeling 130 pounds (59 kilograms) of potatoes and boiling more than 200 pounds (91 kilograms) of rice.

THE LARGEST FAMILY IN THE WORLD

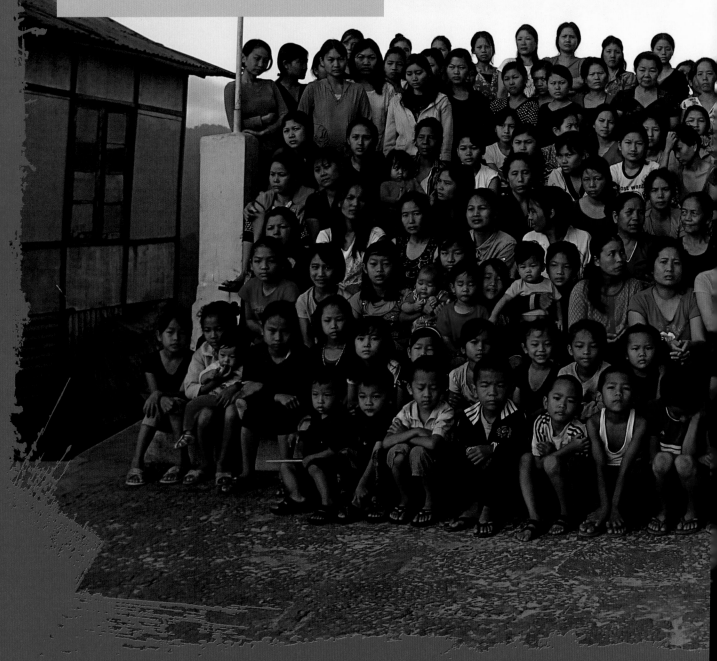

# PEOPLE POWER

One day in the far-flung future, everyone will hold a record for something. These guys have already made their mark, but there's a record out there for everyone …

## ▶ Off His Trolley

https://youtu.be/HcCoVFhdO3g

This crazy record-breaking invention is guaranteed to make the trip to the supermarket a lot more fun. Rodney Rucker of Arizona, USA, has created a shopping trolley 16 feet (4.8 metres) tall and V8-powered – the largest motorized shopping cart in the world. This fantastic vehicle sits six people comfortably in the basket, with another person behind the wheel in the "child's seat". The trolley can comfortably cruise along at 60 mph (96 km/h), but it's probably best not to do that down the frozen vegetable aisle.

## ▶ Heavy Going for Cannonball Juggling

http://y2u.be/KN5i8MPJIVw

Slovakian Milan Roskopf claims 54 official world records in juggling, including juggling chainsaws and juggling upside down. We cannot verify all of them, but this clip was certainly registered as a record. It shows Milan at the Impossibility Challenger festival in Dachau, Germany, where he juggled with three cannonballs for over 15 seconds. It is some feat when you consider that each ball weighs 22 pounds (10 kilograms) – nearly 6.6 pounds (3 kilograms) more than the heaviest ball at your local bowling alley!

## ▶ Hot to Trot

https://youtu.be/8o_pNN3Ndy0

The feat of firewalking, treading bare-footed over burning ashes, has been explained scientifically. Put simply, the amount of time the foot is in contact with the hot surface is minimized in order to prevent the soles of the feet from burning. That said, it's not everyone's idea of fun and many still come away from the activity with burns to their feet. Master firewalker, Scott Bell, braved temperatures of up to 1,300°F (700°C), as he trod a record 328 feet (100 metres) over burning coals – then walked away unharmed.

# ▶ Werewolf Man

http://y2u.be/iGwK67IcUKg

Hypertrichosis – also known as Werewolf Syndrome – is a condition that causes people to sprout thick hair on their faces and bodies. Since the Middle Ages, only 50 people are known to have been affected by this rare complaint – 15 of them in the Gomez family. Of them, Larry Gomez, a Mexican-American actor and circus performer, has been deemed to be the World's Hairiest Man. Apart from his hands and feet, approximately 98 per cent of his body is covered in hair.

THE WORLD'S HAIRIEST MAN

# ▶ Kiss of Death

http://y2u.be/XBb5MQjwr3M

Before he took on this record attempt, part-time snake charmer Thai Khum Chaibuddee warned children and onlookers not to try this stunt themselves. Where he thought they might find 19 King Cobras, let alone want to kiss them, is anyone's guess – their venom can kill a person in 30 minutes. Nevertheless with four snake charmers standing by and a medical team waiting on the sidelines with serum, the fearless Khum Chaibuddee went on to set a new world record by consecutively kissing 19 King Cobras.

# ▶ Deepest Dive

http://y2u.be/8hN1TPCRSWc

Diving in the Red Sea, off the coast of Dahab, Egypt, a South African scuba diver named Ahmed Gabr descended to a world record depth of 1,090 feet 4 inches (332.35 metres), beating the previous record holder by nearly 50 feet. He needed nine tanks of Trimix, a blend of oxygen, nitrogen and helium gases used for deep water dives because, although it took him only around 12 minutes to reach the record depth, he needed 14 hours to return in order to avoid many possible fatal repercussions.

THE WORLD'S DEEPEST DIVE

# RECORD-BREAKING ROBOTS

Science fiction doesn't seem to stay in the films and books for very long these days. Robots, laser guns, super-materials, even robo-bees, are already in the record books.

## Frozen Smoke

https://youtu.be/3bIXUBXj070

Aerogels are the world's lightest solid materials, composed of up to 99.98% air by volume. Created by dehydrating materials such as graphene, scientists can produce a carbon sponge that is 1 inch (2.4cm) square and which weighs just half a milligram and can be balanced on the petals of a flower. Developers claim their "Frozen Smoke" will revolutionize insulation techniques and its ability to absorb up to 900 times its own weight in liquid will surely one day make kitchen paper obsolete.

## ▼ Robo-Bee

https://youtu.be/hEZ7rHRifVc

Scientists in the US have created the World's Smallest Flying Robot based on the anatomy and biology of the bee. The tiny robo-bee, the size of a penny, is built from carbon fibre, weighs a fraction of a gram and has super-fast electric "muscles" to power its wings. Its creators predict these little rob0-bees will be indispensable in the future, used for everything, from monitoring environmental conditions to helping out with search and rescue missions.

THE SMALLEST FLYING ROBOT

# ▼ Metal!!!

https://youtu.be/3RBSkq-_St8

We've got used to seeing weird-looking rock bands, but this is something else. They are called Compressorhead and they play rock covers, including songs by the Ramones and Nirvana. Compressorhead comprises four-armed Stickboy on drums and 79-digited Fingers on guitar, while Bones plays bass. They are all built from scrap metal and they are the World's First Robot Rock Band. They rock as hard as any band, are better behaved (when switched off) and they don't demand drugs and alcohol – just an electric socket and a little oil.

THE WORLD'S FIRST ROBOT BAND

## Laser Beam

http://y2u.be/EzY30Ah8bKY

The laser gun – a firearm we are familiar with from sci-fi films – has finally made its way to reality. This world record of "the most balloons in a single file line consecutively popped from end on with a single fixed visible laser beam" is achieved by a Krypton laser. The laser itself is said to be the world's brightest handheld laser that can be legally owned. It is 8,000 times brighter than the sun and strong enough to point out individual stars in the sky, and be seen in return by astronauts in space.

# SEEING IS BELIEVING

How often do you hear or read of a record and think, "Surely that's just not possible." If only you could see for yourself …

## Tiny Tiger

http://youtu.be/PRM4hsS5h0w

Over 30 years, Taiwanese artist Chen Forng-Shean has amassed a massive body of work, but most of it can be kept in a shoebox. He is an expert in making miniature art, some of which can only be seen through a magnifying glass. He has drawn intricate portraits on a grain of rice; and has a world record for writing on a grain of sand and another for this, the smallest figurine of a tiger, which is about 0.05 inches (1.2 millimetres) long and 0.04 inches (1 millimetre) high.

RECORD-
BREAKING
ROCKERS

## ◀ Rock Record

http://y2u.be/EFEmTsfFL5A

Having Number 1 albums around the world just isn't enough for some bands. In the video for their single 'Ain't It Fun', American rock band Paramore set 10 world records including fastest time to smash 30 guitars with clocks (31.33 seconds); most feathers caught in 30 seconds (18); most vinyl records broken in one minute (58); fastest time to run backwards for 30 feet while holding stuffed animals and wearing a blindfold (6.14 seconds). And, of course, most world records set in a music video (10 world records).

## ▶ Fatal Frog

http://y2u.be/sfENSyycPQ4

They may be just 1–2 inches (2.5–5 centimetres) long, but certain species of the poison dart frog are the most toxic animals in the world. These brightly coloured amphibians are found in the rainforests of Central and South America. Their name comes from the practice of some tribes of lacing their blow-gun arrows with the poison that coats the frog's skin. The golden poison dart frog, for example, contains enough poison to kill 10 adult men.

THE WORLD'S MOST TOXIC CREATURE

## ▼ In the Swim

http://y2u.be/spkjQ3c_AjU

The cheetah is recognized as the fastest animal on earth, but there is one creature who can match it in a race. The Sailfish is the fastest fish in the ocean, because it can swim at speeds around 65 mph (100 km/h). A Sailfish can weigh up to 220 pounds (100 kilograms) and grow up to 10 feet (3 metres) in length, but it reaches such speeds through the water because of its slender body, elongated bill and retractable dorsal fin.

## ◢ Mascot Boogie

http://y2u.be/KEZ35BT2LwQ

Mascots are a big deal in Japan. Everyone from small-town baseball teams to giant corporations has a colourful and loveable *yuru kyara* (meaning "gentle character"). They are so popular that every year, hundreds assemble at a Yuru-Kyara Grand Prix, to crown the country's most popular fluffy friend. In 2013, many of them also took part in a massed dance. 141 joined in, and although seven failed to dance in step with the others, it was enough to secure the Biggest Ever Synchronized Dance by Mascots world record.

# COOL CAR STUNTS

Car stunts are some of the most exciting clips on the site. These drivers risk life and limb to perform incredible record-breaking tricks and skills on four wheels.

## The Ice Cool Driver

http://youtu.be/VW5GMsT32RM

Janne Laitinen is one cool customer. Whereas most of us nervously drive along an icy road at a snail's pace, he puts his foot down and thinks nothing of it. Laitinen is a test driver for Nokian Tyres and in March 2013 he set the world record for fastest car on ice. He took his Audi RS6 up to a speed of 208.602 mph (335.713 km/h) on the natural ice of the Gulf of Bothnia in northern Finland in freezing winter weather.

## ▶ Completely Loopy

http://youtu.be/c6PQ49B5Gpw

Remember the model cars that looped-the-loop on orange tracks on your living room carpet? Now the Hot Wheels toy manufacturers have taken to performing their stunts in real cars. At the 2012 X Games Tanner Foust and Greg Tracy raced through a loop 60 feet (18.3 metres) tall on a death-defying life-size version of the Hot Wheels orange track. Foust, a stuntman in films such as *Fast and Furious: Tokyo Drift* and *Iron Man 2*, said he had to desperately fight blacking out as he experienced around 7Gs of g-force during the stunt.

TWO-CAR
WORLD
RECORD
LOOP

## The Flip Side

http://youtu.be/eh1zrNTPLI0

They call it "sidewall skiing" and it is regarded as one of the most technical driving stunts around. The move involves driving on two wheels through a narrow gap. British stunt driver Dave Ackland set a new world record for skiing, driving a 1968 Vauxhall Viva on two wheels through a gap of 6.6 feet (2.02 metres) – just 26.4 inches (67 centimetres) wider than the height of the car. Ackland drove over a ramp at around 8 mph (12.9 km/h) to flip the vehicle onto its right side wheels, before carefully guiding it between two columns of cardboard boxes.

## ▼ Monster Monster

http://youtu.be/-HtZjUwPiJw

At 11,500 pounds (5,216 kilograms) in weight, 10 feet 6 inches (3.2 metres) tall and riding on 66-inch (167-centimetre) tyres, the legendary monster truck they call Bigfoot was attempting to take back its world long distance jump record. Bigfoot was the original and most famous monster truck, but had not owned the record for 11 years. It was a matter of pride. Finally, in 2012, after a year-long modification, Bigfoot 18 was ready. Driver Dan Runte hit the ramp at 80 mph (129 km/h) and took off...

THE LONG-DISTANCE JUMP RECORD

SMASHING
THE JuMP
RECORD

## ▼ Ramping It Up

http://youtu.be/L5N7R9Wbe_E

This is the closest you will ever come to seeing a flying car. It was New Year's Eve in Long Beach, California in 2009, and 20,000 people had come out to see all-action driver Travis Pastrana try something really crazy. Pastrana, a rally champion turned stunt driver, launched his Subaru Impreza STI rally car off a ramp on the Pine Avenue Pier at 91 mph (146.6 km/h). He soared over Rainbow Harbor before successfully landing on a floating barge 269 feet (82 metres) away – almost 100 feet (30 metres) more than the former jump record.

# PET RECORDS

These cool creatures have been officially verified as the biggest, smallest, cleverest and most agile.

## ▶ Monster Bunny

http://y2u.be/SbADYnhHtGg

Darius the rabbit weighs in at three-and-a-half stone (22.2 kilograms) and is the size of a small child. He's the biggest rabbit in the world, but Darius is no freak. His breed, the Giant Continental, produces large creatures and his mother Alice held the record before him. Five-year-old Darius stretches out to an amazing 4 feet, 4 inches (1.32 metres) long and munches through 4,000 carrots, 120 cabbages and 730 dog bowls of rabbit mix over the year.

**THE WORLD'S BIGGEST RABBIT**

## Who's a Clever Girl Then?

http://y2u.be/unO5whIUF-M

YouTube is full of videos of dogs and sometimes cats performing stunts – but Kili the Senegal Parrot can match them trick for trick. She claims an unofficial world record by pulling off 20 tricks in just under two minutes. Her feats begin with the customary parrot skills such as rope climbing and nodding. Nothing remarkable there, but carry on watching and you'll see Kili go bowling, match rings to pegs and perform a basketball slam dunk. Worthy of the record books, surely?

## ◢ Jump to Conclusions

http://y2u.be/YH-FZFVlB58

Truffles the guinea pig – or, at least, his 13-year-old owner – was determined to finish what he started. In February 2012, the rodent from Fife, Scotland had jumped 12 inches (30 centimetres) from one box to another to set a species record. The world of guinea pig jumping was not going to take this lying down. With over 30 claims appearing for new records, Truffles returned to the fray. Chloe, his owner, set up his boxes and the cucumber, and the King prepared to take back the throne ...

RECORD-BREAKING GUINEA PIG

## Fish for Compliments

http://y2u.be/q1LkR_aeH6A

When you have a goldfish who can swim through hoops, play football, and fetch a ball from the bottom of a tank, who needs a girlfriend? This cruel (if funny) advert features trainer Dean Pomerleau and Albert Einstein II, who has been officially named as the Smartest Fish in the World. Dean has trained Albert to perform these tricks with a feeder stick and certainly questions the myth that goldfish have only a three-second memory.

## ▶ My Little Pony

http://y2u.be/6XQtd9cTGFM

Here's another Einstein. Smaller than most human babies he was just 14 inches (35.5 centimetres) high at birth, weighing only 6 pounds (2.7 kilograms). Now fully grown, Einstein stands 20 inches (50.8 centimetres) high and is officially the World's Smallest Stallion. The smallest horse, Thumbalina, is slightly shorter but unlike her, Einstein is not a dwarf, he is just a mini miniature horse. He does, however, have a big personality. He has his own Facebook page, has appeared on *Oprah* and even has a book written about him.

THE WORLD'S SMALLEST STALLION

# AMAZING WEATHER

More meteorological marvels, including the coldest and rainiest places on Earth, the man who was struck by lightning seven times, almighty sandstorms and the great Chinese floods of 1931.

## Rain Check

http://y2u.be/KmYQxwO2q4g

Cherrapunji, or Sohra, in the Indian state of Meghalaya battles with nearby Mawsynram for the title of the wettest place on Earth. Cherrapunji holds the record for the most rainfall in a calendar month and in a year. It receives rain throughout the year, with 463 inches (11,777 millimetres) of rain fallling annually (compared with an average in England of about 27.5 inches/ 700 millimetres).

## Have You Got Your Vest On?

http://y2u.be/-io4gG6k61c

This two-and-a-half-minute rundown of the five places you might need to wrap up warm visits the globe's extremes: from Arctic points in Canada, Greenland and Russia to Oymyakon in Siberia, the world's coldest inhabited spot. Pride of place, however, goes to a Russian research station on the ice plateau of Central Antarctica. The Vostok station recorded a temperature of -128°F (-89.2°C) in 1983 – still the official record – but in August 2010 a satellite detected nearby pockets of trapped air that dipped as low as –135°F (-93°C).

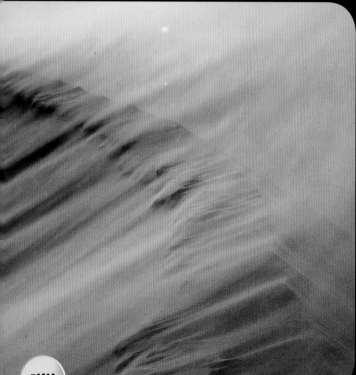

## ◀ Sand-Blasted

http://y2u.be/tiPb-fPujyE

Iran suffers the most sandstorms in the world, as winds gust over its open landscape of dry plateaus, deserts, and salt flats. In 2014, the most devastating sandstorm hit Iran's capital Tehran, killing five people, injuring 30 and bringing chaos to the city. As the freak dust storm rolled through the city, giant clouds of sand and dust clogged the air, plunging the streets into darkness. The storm was accompanied by winds that reached around 75 mph (120 km/ h).

THE WORLD'S WORST SAND-STORM

## ▼ The Greatest Natural Disaster

http://y2u.be/TVB6fuRX6R8

The floods that hit the Republic of China in 1931 make up the deadliest natural disaster ever. A combination of thawing heavy snow, torrential rains and consecutive cyclones caused the Yangtze River to burst its banks. As the rains continued, the country's other major rivers, the Yellow River and the Huai, also flooded. When the waters receded, the damage was estimated to have affected over 28 million people and the death toll to be around four million.

## Lightning Never Strikes Twice

http://y2u.be/bvNayfIrWSc

The only man in the world to be struck by lightning seven times was Roy C. Sullivan, a US park ranger in the Shenandoah National Park in Virginia. Known as "the human lightning conductor", Roy recovered from every one of these strikes, although he did lose a big toe nail, his eyebrows, his hair and suffered many burns. This advert has a bit of fun at his expense but is basically a pretty accurate portrayal of the story of his strikes.

# SPORTS HEROES

From the sublime skills of Cristiano Ronaldo to the stars of quirky sports such as bog snorkling, triathlon juggling and unicycle trampolining, these people are all record heroes.

MULTIPLE FOOTBALL RECORD HOLDER

## Unicycle Trampoline Backflips

http://y2u.be/-XRcXqKu7OI

Canadian Cameron Fraser refers to himself as a contemporary circus artist and after performing feats like this he can call himself whatever he chooses! No one has come near to his achievement of making consecutive backflips while sitting on a unicycle on a trampoline. Cameron manages three complete flips of 360° despite being perched on a unicycle 3 feet (91 centimetres) tall. The feat itself appears around 2 minutes, 10 seconds into this video full of other pretty cool trampolining exploits.

## ▼ Ronaldo's Records

http://y2u.be/KD2NhMPPuf0

As well as being the only League player to score 40 goals in successive seasons, Real Madrid's Cristiano Ronaldo is the player who has scored the highest number of hat-tricks in a single season and has scored in every minute of a game. He is the only player to have won all the major trophies at two different clubs; and, earning a salary of over €20 million per year, he is the highest-paid football player in the world.

## ▼ Ouch!

http://y2u.be/3Sa_3SKiz94

Dr Mak Yuree from Bangladesh is a world-renowned expert in martial arts and an international authority on meditation and mind training. He is probably better known as the man who breaks baseball bats with his tibia. Yuree set a world record shattering three of them in one go, and has since performed the feat on a number of occasions. Sometimes called Thundershin Man, Yuree says he trained for nearly 20 years by kicking tree trunks.

## ▼ Muddy the Waters

http://y2u.be/UoRXZOQBsSQ

The World Bog Snorkelling Championship, first held in 1985, takes place every August at the dense Waen Rhydd peat bog, near Llanwrtyd Wells in mid Wales. Bog snorkelling requires competitors to complete two consecutive 60-yard (55-metre) lengths of a water-filled trench cut through a peat bog. Competitors must wear snorkels and flippers, and complete the course without using conventional swimming strokes, relying on flipper power alone. Andrew Holmes is the record holder with a time of 84 seconds.

## Triathlon Juggling

http://y2u.be/1QoqenZytO8

World record adjudication website Record Setter awarded Joe Salter the Weirdest Record of the Year award in 2012. Joe Salter swam a quarter of a mile (400 metres) while juggling three balls, then cycled 16.2 miles (26 kilometres) while juggling two balls in one hand and also ran 4 miles (6.4 kilometres) while juggling. More incredible still, he managed to do it all in 1 hour, 57 minutes. He threw his balls nearly 20,000 times and managed not to drop a single one while running or on his bike and dropped just three during the swim.

THE WORLD BOG SNORKELLING CHAMPION

## ▼ Cheese Chase

http://y2u.be/xHE3wsQ7Wy0

The Coopers Hill annual event is the oldest Cheese Rolling competition in the world. A 9-pound (4-kilogram) Double Gloucester cheese is chased down the hill. The first person to catch it is the winner. However, since the cheese has a one-second start and reaches speeds of 70 mph (113 km/h), this is usually just a race for the finish. Stephen Gyde is the most successful competitor ever with 21 cheeses and the only competitor to have won all three cheeses in a single year.

CHEESE ROLLING RECORDS

# COOL SPORTS RECORDS

From frantic four-legged running to ninja-powered high kicking, the quest for sporting perfection never ends and with it comes the sound of clattering records.

## Pole Star

http://y2u.be/PwJsmDowiYU

Of all the record breakers in this book, Yelena Isinbayeva is one of the most accomplished. Indisputably the greatest female pole-vaulter of all time, she is a two-time Olympic gold medallist (2004 and 2008), a three-time World Champion (2005, 2007 and 2013) and has broken the world record in the event 28 times. And the sport has existed only since the 1990s! In 2005, Yelena became the first woman to clear 5 metres (16 feet 5 inches), and she then leapt 5.06 metres (16 feet 7 inches) four years later: by now she could well have gone even higher.

FOUR-LEGGED SPRINT RECORD HOLDER

## ▶ Four Legs Good

http://y2u.be/A3rcWarJOe0

Kenici Ito, a 29-year-old man from Tokyo, Japan spent over eight years perfecting a four-legged running style based on the wiry Patas monkey of Africa. Neighbours would see him walking around on all fours and he was even shot at by mistake by hunters when training in the mountains. It all paid off in 2012 when Ito incredibly ran 100 metres in less than 20 seconds. He now runs in four-legged races but admits he is still beaten by a fast dog.

## ▶ Take a Punt

http://y2u.be/Ujg49gZIZz0

High-altitude Denver has been kind to American Football goal kickers over the years, a number of records being set and broken in the thin air. In 2013 Denver Broncos kicker Matt Prater – known as a long if sometimes inaccurate kicker – became the latest to take advantage with a 64-yard (58.5-metre) field goal. Prater is regarded as the perfectionist of the Rugby-style punt. For comparison, see Paul Thorburn's 60-yard (54.9-metre) penalty for Wales against Scotland in 1986 – Rugby's equivalent record.

THE LONGEST AMERICAN FOOTBALL PUNT

## ▲ High Kicking

http://y2u.be/Q8c2-YoLrSs

Taekwondo is a martial art combat and defence discipline which in particular rewards jumping and spinning kicks. The video shows the 23-year-old Colombian fighter Yair Medina setting the world record for a high kick in 2011. His incredible feat requires not only that his foot should reach a height of 9 feet 6 inches (2.9 metres) – higher than a red telephone box – but also that he should have the power to deliver a sharp enough kick to burst a polystyrene plate fixed at that position.

## Sam's Ace

http://y2u.be/uqmy9oxEJig

The Australian Sam Groth is an accomplished professional tennis player. Although never making his mark in the grand slam tournaments, Sam has built a reputation as one of the biggest servers in the game. Playing Uladzimir Ignatik in the 2012 Busan Open Challenger in South Korea, Groth sent down a serve at 163.4 mph (263 km/h), smashing the record of 156 mph (251 km/h) set by Ivo Kalovic. After his defeat to Ignatik, Groth noted that unfortunately hitting the fastest serve didn't mean you win the match.

# WHAT A RECORD!

If God had meant us to fly, he'd have given us wings ...
then again, he did give us skateboards, rollerblades, ramps
and long bungee elastic!

## Water Fall

http://y2u.be/uNXh9gXDd2Y

The Palouse Falls in Washington State stand 17 feet (5.2 metres) taller than Niagara, yet whitewater American kayaker, Tyler Bradt decided to risk his life running the vicious, foaming drop. The 22-year-old American fell 186ft in just 3.7 seconds touching speeds of 100 mph (160 km/h) in the terrifying descent. After plunging underwater about 20 feet (6 metres), Bradt surfaced from the fall's deep pool with a broken paddle, a world record and his only injury, a sprained wrist.

## The Only Way is Down

http://y2u.be/JXyQ3N4S5oc

Marc Sluszny is the most extreme adventurer in the world. He's set a world record in bungee jumping, dived with a Great White Shark and represented Belgium in tennis, fencing, yachting and bobsleigh. In 2012, Marc found a new hobby – running down a building. Here he is completing a vertical run down the side of the Belgacom tower in Brussels. The tower is 335 feet (102 metres) high and he sprinted down the outside of it in a time of 15.5 seconds – a new world record.

## ▶ The "1080"

http://y2u.be/tbjzZHuGTng

In March 2012, at the age of 12, Tom Schaar became a skateboarding legend. Less than a year after becoming the youngest skateboarder (and only the eighth ever) to successfully land a "900" (2.5 revolutions in the air), he landed a three-revolution "1080". He was the first skateboarder to successfully attempt the feat despite many efforts from leading boarders. Tom, who expected to spend all day trying to complete the move, nailed it on only his fifth attempt.

**THE WORLD'S FIRST "1080"**

## ▶ Way Higher, Way Further

http://y2u.be/XNYpV7wtGJ8

Skateboarding legend Danny Way is one of the most accomplished skateboarders of his generation. He was named Skateboarder of the Year twice, won four X Games gold medals, and is the only skateboarder to jump the Great Wall of China. He has had numerous world records and still holds the land speed skateboard record. But surely his greatest feat came in the X Games in 2004.There he broke two records – the Longest and the Highest Air Jump – in one jump. These are records that are still standing 10 years later.

TWO SKATE-BOARDING RECORDS IN ONE

## Elastic Ecstasy

http://y2u.be/zG22qQydPVQ

In 2006 the world's highest bungee jump was installed from the sixty-first floor of the Macau Tower, and bungee pioneer A. J. Hackett was the first to take the plunge. Now it is an extreme sport attraction. Tourists drop from a platform 764 feet (233 metres) high, experiencing freefall of 4–5 seconds as they reach speeds of up to 124 mph (200 km/h). They stretch the 164-foot (50-metre) bungee cord nearly four times its length before beginning the first of several rebounds around 98 feet (30 metres) above the ground.

## Scraping the Barrels

http://y2u.be/Q0qRNiUbdkk

Risking life and limb in ludicrous competition is nothing new. Barrel jumping – vaulting barrels on ice skates – appears to have gone out of fashion amon the adrenaline fanatics despite having the athleticism, skill and obvious danger of broken bones found in modern extreme sports. So we go back to archive footage from the mid-1960s to see Kenneth Lebel clear a then world record of 16 barrels. He actually went on to set the record at 17, but no footage exists of that jump.

# HAIR-RAISING RECORDS

There are some special people for whom "doing their hair" doesn't mean a few minutes with a brush and a mirror. Hairstyles, beards, moustaches and other follicular follies are their step to stardom ...

## ▶ Bearded Lady

http://y2u.be/pn94aT8wsDk

Born with both male and female body parts, doctors operated to allow Vivian Wheeler to live life as a woman. However, she still suffered with a condition known as hypertrichosis or wolf syndrome, in which excessive hair grows on the face. At the age of seven she began shaving and soon was touring as a circus sideshow. Now aged 64 and living in Bakersfield, California, Vivian is the proud owner of the longest female beard – reaching to a majestic 11 inches (27.94 centimetres).

THE WORLD'S HAIRIEST WOMAN

## A Hairy Ride

http://y2u.be/07i3dgB5v44

In 2010 Italian hairstylist Maria Lucia Mugno covered her Fiat 500 in human hair. Maria and her assistant spent 150 hours sewing strands of hair onto the bodywork, seats, dashboard and even the steering wheel. Their efforts earned the title of the World's Hairiest Car, but then in 2014, they added more hair in the shape of butterfly wings. Human hair extensions aren't cheap and the car is now thought to be worth almost £80,000.

THE WORLD'S LONGEST MOHICAN

## ▼ Hard to Handlebar

http://y2u.be/PKzBzDY5I50

Ram Singh Chauhan of India is the proud owner of the world's longest moustache, stretching an incredible 14 feet (4.27 metres). Now 54, he started growing his moustache in 1970. It isn't an easy life – Chauhan spends an hour every day cleaning and combing his moustache and when it is not on proud display, he has to neatly wrap it around his neck. However, it has brought him prestige and some fame, with appearances in Bollywood films as well as the 1983 James Bond film *Octopussy*.

## ▲ The Vast of the Mohicans

http://y2u.be/X__XIPhgH34

Usually Kazuhiro Watanabe's hair is clipped up so it doesn't drag around his knees. It has taken the Japanese fashion designer 15 years to grow it that long, but it is all part of his record-breaking plan. When Kazuhiro gets dressed up (usually for an outdoor event), he and his stylists go to work with three cans of hair spray and an entire bottle of hair gel. Just three hours later, he has the world's highest mohican – a spike that is a massive 3 feet, 8.6 inches (1.13 metres) high.

THE LONGEST MOUSTACHE IN THE WORLD

# SETTING YOUR OWN RECORD

Even in our wildest dreams, we can't hope to emulate the feats of some of the record breakers in this book. The achievements of Usain Bolt or Paul McCartney are the result of a talent and dedication possessed by few. Others are born to be record breakers by dint of an exceptional physical attribute – a long tongue, big feet – whether they like it or not! Still, the budding record breaker need not despair. There are plenty of videos in this book to inspire anyone to write their name in the history books.

Perhaps you already have a unique skill or hobby that can rival the record holders. For example, you might have a great talent for skipping or licking your nose; you might have quick reflexes or a steady hand. It is likely that your particular skill isn't yet at the level of the current record holders; most of the achievements in the book are due to practice and hard graft. Start working at it now, though, and who knows what heights you will reach?

You don't have to possess a great physical skill to enter the record books. There are plenty of other entries that are equally impressive. Mental agility is a popular area and there are incredible feats of reading, mathematics and memory; world-beating collections – of anything from TV show memorabilia to cereal packets – form a fascinating aspect of record-breaking; and someone needs to organize the large-scale gatherings that beat records.

If you need to research your goal, go online and check the existing record. Some in this book did just that and discovered it was a target they could aspire to and eventually beat. There are various organizations, including sporting bodies, who keep their own statistics. Most famously, the Guinness Book of Records (www.guinnessworldrecords.com) has been keeping records since 1955 and has a comprehensive database and an online application process.

If you are looking to set a more unusual record, it might be worth consulting recordsetter.com. Here you will find inspiration and challenges for all kinds of records – many of which can be attempted in your own kitchen or bedroom. If you don't fancy taking on other people's records, you can always invent your own category. You'll definitely have a record, but don't count on keeping the records for long; it's a mighty competitive record-breaking world.

# INDEX

# PICTURE CREDITS

The publishers would like to thank the following sources for their kind permission to reproduce the pictures in this book.

4 AFP Photo/Vano Shlamov/Getty Images, 5 Peter Parks/AFP/Getty Images, 7 Geoffrey Robinson/REX, 8 Professor Splash/Barcroft USA/Getty Images, 9 Felipe Caicedo/AFP/Getty Images, 10-11 Raymond Boyd/Getty Images, 12 Imaginechina/REX, 13 Tinseltown/Shutterstock.com, 14 Shutterstock.com, 15 Matt Cardy/Getty Images, 16 (right) Alexander Hassenstein/Bongarts/Getty Images, (left) Shutterstock.com, 17 (top) Richard Bord/Getty Images, (bottom) Shutterstock.com, 18 Stan Honda/AFP/Getty Images, 19 (top) Shutterstock.com, (bottom) Universal History Archive/UIG via Getty images, 20-23 Shutterstock.com, 24 Bettmann/Corbis, 25 (top) AFP Photo/Vano Shlamov/Getty Images (bottom) Drew Simon/AP/Press Association Images, 26 EPA/Rungroj Yongrit/Corbis, 27 (top) David-Hevia/Demotix/Corbis, (bottom) tipograffias/Shutterstock.com, 28 Ethan Miller/Getty Images, 29 (top) AFP/Getty Images, (bottom) Nick Obank/Barcroft Media / Barcoft Media via Getty Images, 30 (top) Dusso Janladde, (bottom) Ernesto, 31 TowersStreet, 32-33 Shutterstock.com, 34 Fred Duval/FilmMagic, 35-36 Shutterstock.com, 37 (top) Nils Jorgensen/REX, (bottom) Shutterstock.com, 38 Oli Scarff/Getty Images, 39 (top) Shutterstock.com, (bottom) DigitalGlobe via Getty Images, 40 ZUMA Press, Inc/Alamy, 41 (top) Ronaldo Schemidt/AFP/Getty Images, (centre) landmarkmedia/Shutterstock.com, (bottom) Ray Tang/REX, 42-43 Shutterstock.com, 44 Photo by Rauke Schalken with Leica, 45 Hagen Hopkins/Getty Images, 46-47 Arkaprava Ghosh/Barcroft India, 48 Moviestore Collection/REX, 49 (top) Angus Murray /Sports Illustrated/Getty Images, (bottom) Christian Petersen/Getty Images, 50-51 Ray Tang/REX, 52-53 USN Collection/Alamy, 54 Shutterstock, 55 (top) Angela Weiss/Getty Images, (bottom) Shutterstock.com, 56-57 Shutterstock.com, 58 Dan Callister/REX, 59 DFree/Shutterstock.com, 60 East News/REX, 61 (top) Zhukov Oleg/Shutterstock.com, (bottom) Tim Matsui/Getty Images, 62-63 Shutterstock.com, 64 Shutterstock.com, 64-65 Moviestore Collection/REX, 65 Shutterstock.com, 66 (top) Michael Bowles/REX, (bottom) John Springer Collection/Corbis, 67 Universal/Everett/REX, 68 Shutterstock.com, 69 (top) Shutterstock.com, (bottom) Getty Images, 70 Shutterstock.com, 71 (top) AFP Photo/Gent Shkullaku/Getty Images, (bottom) Obuda University, 72 Gonzales Photo/Demotix/Corbis, 73 (top) AFP Photo/Vano Shlamov/Getty Images, (bottom) Shutterstock.com, 74 (top) Eduardo Munoz/Reuters/Corbis, (bottom) Shutterstock.com, 75 (top) AFP Photo/Ben Stansall/Getty Images, (bottom) Shutterstock.com, 76 Julien Warnand/epa/Corbis, 77 (top) Andrea Raffin/Shutterstock.com, (bottom) Yuriy Dyachyshyn/AFP/Getty Images, 78 Shutterstock.com, 79 (top) Laurentiu Garofeanu/Barcroft USA/Barcoft Media via Getty Images, (bottom) Splash News/Corbis, 80 Clodagh Kilcoyne/Getty Images, 81 (top) epa european pressphoto agency b.v./Alamy, (bottom) PTI (Press Trust of India), 82-83 Piti A Sahakorn/LightRocket via Getty Images, 84 Josh Edelson/AFP/Getty Images, 85 (top) Mark Ralston/AFP/Getty Images, (centre) Barry Bland/ Barcroft Media/Getty Images, 86 s_bukley/Shutterstock.com, 87 Con/Demotix/Corbis, 88 Robertus Pudyanto/Getty Images, 89 (top) Shutterstock.com, (bottom) Stacie McChesney/NBC/NBCU Photo Bank via Getty Images, 90 (centre) Shutterstock.com, (bottom) Yamil Lage/AFP/Getty Images, 90-91 Francisco Leong/AFP/Getty Images, 92 Imaginechina/Corbis, 93 (top) Shutterstock.com, (bottom) Gonzales Photo/Demotix/Corbis, 94-95 Liam Cleary/Demotix/Corbis, 96 Ilya S. Savenok/Getty Images, 97 Colorsport/REX, 98-99 Imaginechina/REX, 100 AF archive / Alamy, 101 (top) Ellen DeGeneres, (bottom) Shutterstock.com, 102 Geoffrey Robinson/REX, 103 ZUMA Press, Inc./Alamy, 104 Andrew Savulich/NY Daily News Archive via Getty Images, 105 (top) aberCPC/Alamy, (bottom) Jack Ludlam/Alamy, 106 Shutterstock.com, 107 Steve Russell/Toronto Star via Getty Images, 108-109 Jim Watson/AFP/Getty Images, 110 Rolf Vennenbernd/DPA/Getty Images, 111 Shutterstock.com, 113 HAP/Quirky China News/REX, 114-115 Mark Campbell/REX, 116 Rainer W. Schlegelmilch/Getty Images, 117 (top) Enrique De La Osa/Reuters/Corbis, (bottom) Abel Tumik/Shutterstock.com, 118 Shutterstock.com, 119 ParagonSpaceDevelopment/Splash/Splash News/Corbis, 120 (centre) Eric Sakowski, (bottom) The Bund, 121-122 Shutterstock.com, 123 (top) Ministry of Fisheries via Getty Images, (bottom) Shutterstock.com, 124 NASA, 125 Shutterstock.com, 126 Geraldo Caso/AFP/Getty Images, 127 (left) Shutterstock.com, (bottom) Austral Int./REX, 128 (top) Johan Ordonez/AFP/Getty Images, (bottom) Vent Haven Museum, 129 (top) Shutterstock.com, (bottom) Ulises Ruiz Basurto/epa/Corbis, 130-131 Adnan Abidi/Reuters/Corbis, 132 Shutterstock.com, 133 Moviestore Collection/REX, 134 Harvard's Wyss Institute for Biologically Inspired Engineering, 135 Yoshikazu Tsuno/AFP/Getty Images, 136-137 Shutterstock.com, 138 Jeff Gross/Getty Images, 139 Tim Defrisco/Getty Images, 140-141 Garth Milan/Red Bull Photofiles via Getty Images, 142 Caters News Agency, 143 (top) Shutterstock, (bottom) Katie Greene/Bellingham Herald/MCT via Getty Images, 144 Shutterstock.com, 145 Topical Press Agency/Hulton Archive/Getty Images, 146 Marcos Mesa Sam Wordley/Shutterstock.com, 147 REX, 148-149 Justin Tallis/AFP/Getty Images, 150 Toru Yamanaka/AFP/Getty Images, 151 (top) Justin Edmonds/Getty Images, (centre) Shutterstock.com, 152 AFP Photo/Peter Parks/Getty Images, 153 Harry How/Getty Images, 154 KeystoneUSA-ZUMA/REX, 155 (left) Adrees Latif/Reuters/Corbis, (right) Arkaprava Ghosh/Barcroft India, 160 HAP/Quirky China News/REX

Every effort has been made to acknowledge correctly and contact the source and/or copyright holder of each picture and Carlton Books Limited apologizes for any unintentional errors or omissions, which will be corrected in future editions of this book.